# Indian Politics Vs. Indian Constitution

Hari Babu E

INDIA • SINGAPORE • MALAYSIA

ISBN  978-1-63745-332-2

# Contents

Contents

# Introduction

Dear Readers!

Please read this book and you would sure respond!

Indian constitution was drafted by several committees under the chairmanship of Dr. Ambedkar, which task took nearly 3 years. Hence, probably, all the members did not have comprehensive understanding of the scheme of the constitution. Ambedkar could be having total knowledge of it, but he became voiceless when his party Scheduled Castes Federation got just 2.38 percent of polled and valid votes and he himself lost the election in the First general Elections of 1952 while congress party under Nehru got about 360 seats or about 70 percent of seats in the Lok Sabha. Ambedkar changed the name of his party as Republic Party of India in Octoer 1956, but died in December. As a result, Bharathiya Constitution was totally ignored by rest of the polity of those days. Today's social strife, poverty and political instability in the country are the results of ignoring the constitution. Leaders have just ignored the constitution. I have no hesitation to hold that all sections of the country are misled on all important characteristics of the constitution.

Bharath has all the natural, human and tourist resources required to make it the best in the world. What it lacked is an honoured constitution. Indian politics are moving by default, but not by design of the constitution. Bharathiya constitution is still capable of turning Bharath in to a stable political and financial force in the world. It is time to read and implement it at once or else, the country is bound to lose its sovereignty, unity, and integrity in due course. I bring some of such issues to your knowledge through this book.

Sincerely yours,

Hari Babu E, Advocate

Hyderabad, Telangana, 15-8-2023.

# 1

# Call Your Country "Bharath"

Article 1 of the Constitution declared, "India that is Bharath shall be a Union of states." In "India that is Bharath," India is a referring or describing word while Bharath is the name proper of this country. If the constitutional framers wanted to call this country as India, they would have not used the word, Bharath at all.

India, was a vast area ruled by the British which was also referred to as British India out of which, several countries have emanated post-independence and adopted their own cherished names which reminisce their own culture, history, identity, and ideology. It is misfortune of this country that it is still called India despite the constitution named it as Bharah. Once you say "India that is Bharath," you need not utter the word India again and again. You should always call this country only as "Bharath."

The word Bharath denotes a lot to its denizens regarding their past glory, culture, knowledge, traditions, and history. It is evocative of lot of lore of yore of which each Bharathiya would feel proud. It reminisces every citizen, the names of several native kings and their ruling, saints and their preachings, monuments and their glories, scientists and their knowledge and reformers and their sacrifices. It is believed that this name "Bharath" was derived because king Bharath once ruled this country which extended among four oceans. He was supposed to be the ancestor of Kauravas and Pandavas, who ruled about 5300 years ago. Their ancestor, namely, Bharath must have existed much prior to that.

We have not gained back, through so called independence of 1947, what we have lost for centuries and for which we fought for one hundred years and sacrificed several lacks of lives in that process, namely, the national pride.

Independence does not mean a few rations, pensions and reservations or physical facilities which the birds in poultry sheds get more in the form of food and shelter, medicine, and transportation devoid of any thing of their own to be proud of.

No conscious effort was made to reestablish the Bharathiya national identity or Bharathiyatha after gaining independence. The centuries old Bharathiya culture and knowledge, which was suppressed for thousands of years by foreign rulers, has been dealt with a death blow instead of nurturing it with care and compassion. Native leaders of this country destroyed more of national fabric during the last 75 years than the foreigners did in the last several centuries.

If nationalism does not flourish in the country, the country is bound to lose its nationhood and become just a landed part of another country in due course of time. If a culture is lost, the persons nurturing it would become individuals living for food, cloth, and shelter devoid of any history or pride, tradition, culture, language, knowledge, or values of their own. Thus, Bharath will not be a nation if there is no fraternity and individual dignity in it, as enshrined in the Preamble.

The feeling of Bharathiyatha will continue to influence its native population for long whether they live in this country or abroad, whichever faith they follow. People who migrated to other countries from Bharath for employment or for whatever reasons, are not subject to Bharathiya sovereignty. Yet, they observe Bharathiya festivals, teach their children their mother language, train them in Bharathiya art forms, clad their children in traditional attire on festivals and feel gratified. The traces of Bharathiyatha lie in this trait of Bharathiya people, where ever they live.

In case of a country, the geographic area is its body, sovereignty is its life and the feeling of Bharathiyatha or nationalism that nurtures in the hearts of people is its soul. "Bharathiyatha" is the rich and varied cultural heritage evolved over times immemorial. We should adhere to it with veneration and pride.

Bharathiyatha does not relate to any religion exclusively. It encompasses all walks of life of people lived and living in this country. If this feeling of "Bharatheeya" is alive in the hearts of people, freedom will be regained as many times as it may be lost to others. If such feeling is not nurtured in the hearts of people, there would not be freedom struggles anymore in future even if freedom of the country is lost.

Whoever are in whichever faith, they should honour the ancient glory, culture, traditions, texts, and knowledge of ancient Bharath because it is this characteristic that distinguishes the country and every inhabitant in it from rest of the world. This was also the culture followed by their forefathers. Religious faith should be distinguished from their race and nationalism.

Beliefs, principles, and practices of all faiths being uniform to a great extent, vindicate that all religions emanated from the same basic knowledge, principles, and practices at different parts of the world during different times. Religious and social practices vary to some extent because they flourished in different parts of the world where the languages, weathers, foods, and some existing practices specific to each race and region also vary. This is also the way other societies in the world look at Bharathiyas. They consider every citizen of this country as Bharathiya.

A person's religion may be changed in a split second if his faith changes but his nationality cannot change at his choice. As such, every Bharathiya should strive to achieve value in the name of his nationality. Religions are imaginary, and fragile. Unless politicians incite religion against religion, people do not fight among themselves in the name of their religions.

We should not forget that Hindus, Sikhs, Muslims, Christians and all other castes and religions together fought to gain independence from the British because they considered this land as their mother land.

Even if Bharathiya rulers lose sovereignty, people should not lose the character of being Bharathiya which denotes their ancestral and historical pride. It is beyond politics and runs in the blood of people through generations. It distinguishes us from the rest of the world. It is for the citizens of a state to protect and enhance value for their nationality. Whether a culture remains alive through centuries of vagaries of wars and aggressions, social and political, depends upon the integrity and ability of the members consisting in that culture.

One of my friends questioned me "What is in name? We need development". This was a pretentiously innocent question. I told him that his parents named him Johnson, why? They wanted that the name of their child should denote his social and cultural identity. So, should be the name of a country. Changing of the name of the country would not be an impediment in the economic development of the country. On the other hand, it promotes nationalism with pride. Bharath belongs to all religions existing in the country. Bharath is a national concept in contrast with concept of religious faith of individuals which is subject to change.

# 2

# America Is Federal: Bharat Is Not

America is expressly Federal by its Constitution. Its states have their own Constitutions, own flags, ruled by elected Governors. The President and the Congress have no right to alter names, extent, and status of states. American Union government is called Federal government. States in America enjoy independence to some extent which is a federal feature. America is Federal and Presidential Democracy having an elected President unlike U.K. which is a Parliamentary Democracy. American constitution took every care befitting that of a federal structure to see that secessionist forces would not usurp. Federal government exercises total command over the entire country in all important matters concerning the country.

Great Briton is Parliamentary Democracy with Parliament elected Prime Minister and a hereditary King. Briton does not have an elected President like America and the Bharath. Briton does not have a written constitution and runs on Parliamentary practices which is called West Minister Style of governance. Briton is neither politically stable nor economically prospering with their systems despite being a country which ruled half of the globe in the past. Adopting the British model is neither legal nor does it do any good for Bharath.

Pakistan Constitution described that country as Federal Republic, but it does not have Unitary, Federal, Republican, or even Democratic features in full because Prime Minister is empowered under its constitution to dismiss Parliament midterm and Chief Ministers are empowered to dismiss assemblies midterm. Prime Minister is elected by the Parliament alone, while the President is elected by the Parliament and all the assemblies in Pakistan. Yet, Prime Minister commands the President according to their constitution. It is not any sound logic. It contained several Articles akin to Bharatiya Constitution but modified them with conjunctions such as "but, however" etc. and added whatever they wanted at the end of each Article. Irony is that, Bharath is following those additions made in the Pakistan constitution though such additions are not contained in the Bharatiya constitution.

For example, Article 75 of Indian constitution states that the Prime Minister is appointed by the President. Pakistan constitution says that the President shall appoint a parliament member as Prime Minister after ascertaining his majority in the parliament. In terms of Indian constitution, the term of office of

Prime Minister shall be during the pleasure of the President.. Pakistan constitution added a rider to it as "however, the President shall not exercise his option without conducting a no-confidence motion in the parliament.

It is only a misnomer to call Bharath as Federal. The central ministers are called the Union ministers or combinedly the Union cabinet and the government, Union government. It is neither federal government nor the ministers, federal ministers. "Uni" denotes oneness. Bharath is Sovereign Democratic Republic as per the Preamble and Union of States as per Article 1. Union of States, means, and denotes unified states as constituting Bharath. The word "Federal" was rejected by Dr. Ambedkar and the constituent assembly.

K.T. Shah, a Socialist member in the Constituent Assembly, during constitutional debates, proposed to add "Socialist, Secular and Federal" in to the preamble to which Ambedkar stoutly opposed and succeeded in stalling the proposal of Shah. Hence, calling Bharath "Federal" or inserting Socialist and Secular in to the Preamble is an insult to him. "Socialist and Secular" are the communistic features existing in China and Russia.

42$^{nd}$ constitutional amendment of 1976 added "Secular and Socialist" but not "Federal" in to the preamble. Nevertheless, Nehru administered the country in Socialist, Secular and Federal pattern without adding these words in to the Preamble. Indira Gandhi went a step ahead and added Socialist and Secular in to the preamble to lend legality to the policy of her father. After this addition, Bharath became "Sovereign Socialist Secular Democratic Republic." However, amending the Preamble, the objects clause of the constitution, under Article 368 is illegal. Especially, incompatible objectives cannot be clubbed together in it. People who call Bharath "Federal," should think over as to wherefrom and why they brough this word "Federal" in to picture and whether they have such right.

Whether a country is federal or unitary, the first and foremost objective of its constitution shall be to keep the country unified and integral; not to disintegrate it. A country to be federal, its states should have independent rights and existence, but be bound strongly to form a single country like America. If you draft the constitution for a Unitary structure and follow federalism in practice, there would always be conflicts between states and states and states and the centre which ultimately lead to political turmoil and bifurcation of the country.

# 3

# Bharath Is Presidential Democracy, Not Parliamentary.

Bharath is Union of States and a Republic by its constitution. President is the only elected Executive in Bharath. Hence, it is Unitary. Union ministers are appointed by him to aid and advise him in executing his functions and to hold office during his pleasure under Articles 74 and 75. Under Articles 155 and 156, President appoints Governors to hold office during his pleasure.

In the states, ministers are appointed by the Governors to aid and advise them in executing their functions and to hold office during pleasure of the Governors under Articles 163 and 164. Republic means, a country, to be ruled by an elected or nominated President instead of a monarch, in which people are supreme.

Entire Bharathiya constitution was couched to realize this objective which has been totally ignored ever since the beginning by Bharathiya politicians for their own reasons: connivance or ignorance. America and Bharath have Electoral college elected Presidents in contrast with the Great Briton which has elected Prime Minister.

Article 324 prescribed only two elections in Bharath: General elections to the legislatures and the election of the Executive namely, the President. No other election is recognized by the constitution regarding the legislative and the Executive.

President appoints the Judiciary and certain other constitutional authorities like the Attorney General, Auditor General, Election Commission and various other Commissions to discharge certain constitutional functions. This is the Unitary form of governance envisaged under the constitution for harmonious ruling of the states and the centre without conflicts among them.

There would be NDA governments at the centre and in the states when President of Bharath is elected from NDA and vice versa, irrespective of majorities of political parties in each of the assemblies and in the Parliament. If this constitutional prescription is followed, there would never be disputes between centre and the states, states and the states. Polity would be stable because President cannot be impeached by the Parliament under Article 161 unless he violated the constitution. Central and state legislatures run invariably for five years under Bharathiya constitution. There would never be midterm elections to them. However, there may be midterm elections to the post of President due to his death, resignation, retirement or impeachment.

To describe Bharatiya constitutional political system, it is an "Umbrella Model". The centre pole is the union government while the spokes, hanging around through hinges, are the state governments and the top cover is the constitution. The authority holding the umbrella is the President, elected by the legislators. He takes care of the constitution, law, and welfare of the citizens under the umbrella. Unfortunately, at present, the authority who should hold the umbrella, firm, is made infirm due to which the umbrella is blown off by unethical political winds and the people remained unprotected while the President remained silent spectator.

Majority in Lok Sabha or in states' assemblies has nothing to do with forming government at the centre or in the states by the Executive. Ministers are not necessarily elected members of legislatures. They could be nominated members to the councils. For six months after being appointed as ministers, they may not be even nominated or elected members. In my opinion, they can be reappointed as ministers every six months. The Hon'ble Supreme Court held otherwise in S.R. Chowdhury case, but I do not find sound logic in it. Even Ambedkar was against such opinion when he said that winning of elections was totally different from one's ability to aid and advise the Executive.

Forming governments at the centre or in the states based on majority in Lok Sabha or Assembly leads to dictatorship because the same political party or coalition of political parties make law and enforce it which resembles the power of monarch. It leads to oppression of the opposition parties; it defies doctrine of separation of powers among the Executive, the Legislative and the Judiciary. You can witness such happenings in some of the Bharathiya states where the opposition parties are suffering at the hands of the ruling party.

In some states, on the day of counting of votes itself, defeated party leaders' houses may be razed, their women raped, businesses destroyed, they may be beaten up by police and the political workers, they may be put behind bars for trivial or bogus reasons. In some states, opposition is demolished and draconian laws passed in the legislatures. Sometimes, the opposition is suspended from the legislatures and thrown out by marshals and bills passed by the governments. I think, this is the punishment they deserve for not understanding what separation of powers is in a democracy.

American President is indirectly elected by the Electoral College consisting of Electors who are elected by the people for that purpose and hence, he may or may not hold majority in any or both houses of Parliament and other state assemblies. American Congress members participate in Presidential elections only when there is a tie in the votes of Electors. Legislative power of America is vested in the Congress while the Executive Power of America is vested in the President of America. America is the best example of Presidential Democracy, Federalism and separation of powers.

Bharathiya President too is indirectly elected by the Electoral College consisting of the elected members of all the assemblies and both houses of the Parliament and hence, he too may or may not hold majority in either or both houses of Parliament and several other state assemblies. It should not impede his Executive Power to rule the country. Majority in houses is necessary for making laws, but not for implementing them by the Executive.

In Bharath, Executive Power of Union is vested in the President under Article 53 and that of the states is vested in the Governors, under Article 154. Legislative Power of Union is vested in the parliament and that of states is vested in the legislatures of respective states. However, introduction and passing of money bills is exclusive business of the Lok Sabha and Assemblies, to the exclusion of central and state Councils.

In America, term of House of Representatives is 2 years; that of President is 4 years; that of Senators is 6 years. Elections to the Congress would invariably take place twice during the term of office of the President. In such elections, he may not get majority yet, neither his Executive Power diminishes nor is he impeached.

In Bharath too, the term of state and central legislatures was 6 years under Articles 83 and 172 which was reduced to 5 years through 42nd amendment in 1976. The term of council of states is 6 years. The term of office of President is 5 years under Article 56. Thus, general elections to the legislatures and elections to the post of President would never have taken place simultaneously and the composition of legislatures that takes place after each general elections would not result in change of the President. Even in the present context in Bharath, election of the President and elections to the legislatures would not happen simultaneously. They take place at different times due to resignation, retirement, death, or impeachment of the President.

Unfortunately, Bharathiya leaders made mess of democracy. Legislatures are not only making laws, but also electing Prime Minister and the chief Ministers who are also exercising Legislative, Executive and to a great extent Judicial and Quasi-judicial powers. All government officers of certain rank exercise Judicial and Quasi-judicial powers. Once after coming to power, they can demolish the oppositions by hook or crook and pass draconian laws. Democracy disappears. It is dangerous for the people, for the opposition parties, for the state and for the country.

Political parties are electing their Parliamentary party leaders in the Lok Sabha and Legislative party leaders in the respective assemblies. They are being appointed as Prime Minister by the President. Majority party leader in the Assembly is being appointed as Chief Minister by the Governor. In that process, to prove their majority in the houses, aspiring leaders are kidnapping and hiding legislative members to prevent their being poached by other parties. When these kidnapped legislators are presented before the executive by the aspiring candidates, to prove their majority, supporting political parties issue Whip to their members to ensure that they vote openly and as per directions of the party because, the members and their party leaders would have been heavily paid or promised ministerial berths for supporting the aspiring candidates to become Prime Minister or a Chief Minister. They are all false, funny, and shameful practices which do not constitute democracy; neither are they prescribed in the constitution.

Every party may elect their leader which is their party affair to be conducted in their party office. Lok Sabha or assemblies have nothing to do with such elections. Constitution does not recognize such elections.

We see, sometimes, somebody who is not member of the house is appointed Prime Minister or Chief Minister by the President or the Governors as the case may be, at the behest of a majority political party or majority coalition of political parties, but it is an unconstitutional practice. It is not legally correct to say that a political party can chose somebody who is not member of the legislatures as their Parliamentary party leader or as legislative party leader. A person who is not member of a cricket team cannot be its captain. He can at best be the coach or the manager of the team who should stay out of the court and guide the players at times of intervals. Team members may go to him, take his advice, and follow it, but cannot invite him to enter in to the playing arena. The same way, any person before becoming member of the legislatures cannot enter the house or take seat in it at the behest of a political party. It is the right of the Executive to appoint any one including a non-member as minister. Conditions such as appointing some member of the house by the President after ascertaining his majority in the house and to remove him after he lost majority, as proved in a no-confidence motion, are not contained in Bharathiya constitution. They are contained in Pakistan constitution under Articles 91, 95 and 130.

A Republic is always democratic because the President is elected by the public or by their representatives. It would have been sufficient for the constitutional framers to describe Bharath as Republic in the preamble. The rhetoric words such as Sovereign Democratic Republic confused the people of Bharath and led them to miss the true purport of those words.

In S.R. Bommai, 1994 case, Hon'ble Supreme Court held that Bharath was federal and that popular governments in the states should survive. Both the propositions made by the court in this case were against the constitution in as much as Bharath was Unitary and Republic as explained in the foregoing chapters.

In Shamsher Singh and another Vs Government of Punjab, in 1972 Hon'ble Supreme Court made a remark that President was "elected on a limited indirect basis". Their Lordships failed to appreciate that the President was the only elected Executive in Bharath by the electoral college, through an elaborate electoral process, under Articles 54 and 55. Prime Minister and Chief Ministers are not elected at all, directly or indirectly.

# 4

# Pakistan Constitution, Being Followed in Bharath

Unfortunately, Pakistan Model of government is being implemented in Bharath against its own constitution. Pakistan is Federal Republic by Preamble of its constitution. Bharath is Sovereign Democratic Republic and Union of states. Surprisingly, what is taking place in Bharath, in the Executive and Legislative spheres, in the name of Bharathiya constitution, is comparable with what is stated in the Pakistani Constitution of 1973.

Pakistan constitution, Article 42, states that Oaths of office of President, Prime Minister and other Ministers shall be as listed in Schedule 3. They undertake to "Preserve, Protect and Defend the constitution." In Bharath, President and Governors alone take such oath under Articles 60 and 159 while all others take oath, as contained in Schedule 3, to bear true allegiance to the constitution and to uphold the Sovereignty, Unity, and Integrity of the country.

It is the Federal government which commands armed forces in Pakistan under Article 243 and not the President. The Pakistani President is commander of armed forces, but he must act according to advice of the Prime Minister.

Bharathiya President is the supreme commander of armed forces under Article 53 which post he shall exercise in accordance with law made for that purpose. We know, in Bharath, any law is made only after assent of the President.

Pakistani President may be removed under Article 47 for gross misconduct or violating the constitution. Bharathiya President cannot be impeached under Article 61 unless he violated the constitution. Misconduct is a subjective term while violation of the constitution, a legal incident, a judiciable term. Bharathiya constitution provides for constitution of special Tribunal to decide whether the President violated the constitution or not.

Under Article 48, in exercise of his functions, the President of Pakistan shall act in accordance with the advice of the cabinet or the Prime Minister. Bharathiya constitution originally did not contain such provisions under Articles 74 or under any other provisions. It was only in 1976 that such provision was incorporated in Article 74 through 42nd amendment by Indira Gandhi to lend legality to the unconstitutional practice initiated by her father in 1950 and continued till then.

In Pakistan, under Article 58, The President shall dissolve the Parliament on the advice of the Prime Minister. If the President does not do that earlier, the Parliament shall be deemed dissolved at the expiration of 48 hours from the time of advice by the Prime Minister and the President shall cause elections to be held within 90 days after dissolution of Parliament. Bharathiya constitution does not have explicit provisions to this effect; but the irony is that Bharathiya President is pedantically following the advice of the cabinet to dissolve House of the People or the assemblies and to hold midterm elections to the legislatures within 6 months.

In Pakistan, under Article 90, the executive power of federal government shall be exercised in the name of the President by the Prime Minister. Prime Minister shall be the chief executive of the federation. This is also what has been happening in Bharath ever since beginning though the opposite is stated in the Bharathiya constitution under Article 53, and 77.

Under Article 91 and 95, the President of Pakistan shall appoint a Parliament member as Prime Minister who, in his opinion, commands majority in the Parliament. He shall convene a joint session to ascertain majority. Pakistani Prime Minister shall hold office during the pleasure of President who shall not exercise his option without ascertaining majority in the Parliament through no confidence motion. Such provisions, as ascertaining of majority in Lok Sabha or both houses of parliament or conducting of no-confidence motions in the Lok Sabha or the Parliament, for appointment or removal of Prime Minister, are not contained under Bharathiya

Constitution. Bharathiya Executive can appoint even non-members as ministers.

In Pakistan, under Article 101, state Governors are appointed by the President on the advice of the Prime Minister to hold office during pleasure of President. In Bharath, Prime Minister is not given such power under any provisions of the constitution, but an unwritten law is being followed in Bharath. In Bharath, Governors are appointed by the President under warrant to hold office during the pleasure of the President under Articles 155 and 156.

In Pakistan, under Article 105, Governors shall act on the advice of the Chief Ministers or the cabinet. Under Article 112 of their constitution, Governor shall dissolve Assembly within 48 hours of receiving advice from the Chief Minister to do so. If he does not do that, the Assembly stands dissolved after 48 hours of advice by the Chief Minister. Re-elections would be held within 90 days. In Bharath, Article 163 (2) specifically states that Governors shall act independently and that his discretions shall not be questioned. In terms of Article 163, ministers are not supposed to advise the Governor in functions which require his own discretion. Whether a Governor acted in his discretion or on advice of ministers is not questionable. In terms of Article 166, a Governor is not supposed to delegate to ministers such functions which require his own discretion.

Bharathiya President is more like American President and much more; Bharathiya Governors are his agents. Bharathiya Ministers are his assistants. We have copied sections of American constitution; not of Pakistan! Bharathiya President is bestowed with more executive, administrative, legislative, financial, and judicial powers to run the country as unitary than his American or Pakistan counter parts. The God alone should know as to why we are following Pakistan model of government while neglecting our own constitution.

As in Bharath, Pakistan President is elected by the Electoral College consisting of Parliament members and the assemblies in terms of Article 41 of their constitution while their Prime Minister is elected by the Parliament members alone. Both are indirectly elected. Pakistan people also should ponder over as to why the Parliament elect Prime Minister should have all the powers as against the President who is elected by the Parliament and all the assemblies as well.

We are witnessing the ill effects of lapses of Pakistan constitution. Several Prime Ministers were dismissed, imprisoned, exiled, hanged, and killed. None completed 5year term. Terror is ruling the roost. India too is suffering with the same problems because of following Pakistan constitution. Instead, I may say, Pakistan, Bangladesh, Nepal, Srilanka etc., several countries are suffering political instability due to their copying provisions of Indian constitution in to theirs.

If Bharath and Pakistan people understand their constitutions in their right perspective, both countries would flourish in all aspects and enjoy political stability. There would not be vote bank politics. A legal and tolerant society for mutual coexistence could have emerged. After all, all the citizens of this region would have been blood relatives to each other for thousands of years before each of them changed their faiths regarding the God and started living in different countries due to political reasons.

# 5

# Legislative Majority Rule Is Jungle Law; Not Democracy

Cardinal principle of democracy is separation of powers between the Legislative, the Executive and the Judiciary which is missing in Bharath. If all or any two powers are vested in one person or agency, it would be tyranny.

In wars for the crowns, lacs of soldiers were killed on both sides. Winning soldiers committed loot, arson, rape and mayhem on the citizens of lost kingdoms with vengeance and retribution. Whoever surrendered were enslaved. Kings were beheaded and their treasuries and crowns were grabbed, their young wives and daughters were taken away forcefully, entire clan is annihilated.

As a shift from Monarchy to Democracy, several democratic countries adopted this principle. In the good olden days of monarchies, all the three used to be reposed in the king himself which led to tyranny. Whoever were against the king were branded traitors and beheaded. The situation has changed with advent of democracies in the world. Bharath is not able to enjoy the fruits of democracy as handed over by the constitution due to ignorance or malevolence.

In Bharath, Constitution is superior and binding on all the three: legislative, Executive and the judiciary. The constitution cannot be amended under Article 368 unless, both, Legislatures and the Executive are in consensus. All the three must function within the constitutional contours.

Legislatures are superior as far as legislative functions are concerned. The Executive is bound to assent to bills passed in the houses if they are not against the constitution or law, under Article 111, 200 or a constitutional amendment under Article 368. At the most, the Executive may return the bill for reconsideration of the legislatures, for a single time. If the bill is passed again with or without modifications, if the bill is not against the constitution or other law, the Executive is bound to assent to it. This is the strength of legislatures as far as legislative functions are concerned. The job of legislatures is to participate in Presidential elections and make law for the country. It is misnomer that governments make law. It is the legislatures which make law even if they are filled by opposition parties. The Executive would assent to valid bills passed by opposition parties whereupon they become law. If the Executive holds majority in the legislatures, it is not a good democracy. Opposition should be strong in a democracy.

Executive is superior as regards Executive functions are concerned. The Executive can withhold unconstitutional or illegal bills though passed in the legislatures. State and central government employees are their subordinates under Article 310. Government employees are the Executive in Public Service mentioned in Article 50. Ministers are also subordinates to the Executive, with duty to aid and advise the Executive, but they are like casual labour. Parliament cannot impeach the President unless he violated the constitution under Article 61. Even if he violated the constitution, he cannot be impeached without two thirds majority in both houses of the parliament separately. Under Article 361, the courts are not empowered to summon the Executive to the courts.

Judiciary is superior as regards judicial functions are concerned. They have to dispense justice without fear or favour in accordance with the laid down law. Their appointment, transfer etc., are dealt with by none other than the President. Regarding their removal, Judges cannot be impeached by the President at his pleasure as he could do in matters of ministers and governors. It requires sanction of the parliament. This is the kind of independence and protection which is provided to the judiciary under the constitution.

The purpose of all the four wings of democracy namely Legislative, Executive, Judiciary and the Bureaucracy is to safeguard the Sovereignty, unity, integrity, individual dignity, and welfare of the citizens. If these objectives are under threat, the Executive is empowered to do anything to save the situation.

Union ministers are collectively answerable to the Parliament under Article 75 and the state ministers are collectively answerable to the respective assemblies under Article 164. If majority party in the houses forms council of ministers, as is now happening, the statement that council of ministers is answerable to the legislatures, is as good as saying that the council of ministers shall be answerable to the political party to which they belong, a meaningless statement! Ministers are collectively answerable to the legislatures which contains opposition parties, on behalf of the President as his subordinates.

People are supreme in a Republic. Final authority is kept in the hands of the people in the form of voting in the elections every five years which decide who should be the Executive and who should be the Legislative at the Centre and in States. They judge the legislative and the Executive and vote accordingly. They change the legislators through their vote in the election which in turn would change the Executive. In my opinion, the hierarchy in a democracy is 1) the people, 2) the constitution, 3) the President, 4) the Legislatures, 5) the Judiciary and 6) the Bureaucracy.

These are the checks and balances incorporated in the Bharathiya constitution to regulate the functions of the Legislatures, Executive, the Judiciary, and the Bureaucracy to secure wellbeing of the people and to secure the sovereignty of the country. Bharathiyas failed to understand the fine points of the constitution and of the democracy and destroyed both altogether.

# 6

# First Leaders misled Bharath, Next Leaders Wrongly Ratified

Nehru assumed charge as Prime Minister in 1947 according to the British conventions. Irony is that the same system is continuing till date to utter disregard of the constitution which came in to existence on 26th January 1950. Since the same party ruled this country for 30 years from 1947 till 1977, none questioned the propriety of Prime Ministerial rule and it has got established as practice by precedence.

There was ad hoc government From 1947 to 1952, Nehru as Prime Minister. First general elections were held in 1952. Ambedkar's party "Scheduled Castes Federation of India" polled just 2.38% of polled and valid votes and he, himself lost the election while congress party, under Nehru, got 45% votes and 75% of Lok Sabha seats. Ambedkar became voiceless. He renamed his party as "Republic Party of India" in October 1956 which was proof of his knowledge that Bharath be ruled as Republic by President and not by Prime Minister. He, however, died in December 1956 without facing Second general elections of 1957.

Indira Gandhi lost 1977 elections, to Janata coalition. It was a golden opportunity at that time in the hands of Janata Party to shift to Presidential form of governance by electing a new President in as much as the term of the then President of Bharath, Dr. Fakhruddin Ali Ahmed had just ended due to his death and it coincided with the general elections of 1977. Janata coalition Party has not utilized this opportunity. Instead, they followed the foot prints of Congress party in establishing of Prime Minister led government. It also followed the same wrong path of dissolving the House of the People and conducting of midterm elections to it in 1980.

In 1977, Morarji Desai was chosen to be Prime Minister and Sanjeev Reddy, to be President. Had they realized real powers of President of Bharath; they would have not fought for the post of termless and powerless Prime Minister. Had they chosen Morarji Desai to be President of the country, Janata government would have not fallen midterm because the term of office of President is 5 years in terms of Article 56. However, they fought among themselves for the post of Prime Minister and successfully brought down their own government. In the midterm elections that ensued, Congress emerged as party with clear majority in House of the People and the Janata coalition parties disappeared from the political scenario of the country with satisfaction that none of their colleagues could become Prime Ministers, at least. After midterm elections of 1980, Indira Gandhi took over as Prime Minister as leader of majority party in the House of the People, as was in practice till then. Nevertheless, it was an unconstitutional method of becoming Prime Minister.

Indira Gandhi, instead of taking over as Prime Minister in 1980, she should have waited being in opposition and become President herself in 1982, after the term of Sanjeev Reddy, and rule the country with full Constitutional prescription. But she faced the same predicament as was faced by her father in 1950. If powers of President were acknowledged in 1980, Sanjeev Reddy would have taken reigns of the government and appointed his own ministers and rule the country, to the exclusion of Congress party, until his term ended in 1982. Who should be his ministers would have been his choice.

If Sanjeev Reddy tried to exercise his powers as President in 1980, he could be impeached by Congress party because he committed the constitutional violation of dissolving the house mid-term based on advice of the then Prime Minister, Charan Singh, though the constitution did not provide for dismissal of Lok Sabha, midterm. Indira Gandhi, having committed the same sin of advising the President to dismiss House of the People in 1971, remained silent on that issue and continued the Prime Ministerial set up which, none other than her father established in 1947. If she tried to impeach the President for dismissing the House of the People, or tried to establish unitary and Republic form of governance, she would be contradicting the practices established by her own father which amounts to accepting guilt of her party and of her father which she could not do under any circumstances. Thus, hypocrisy and ignorance ruled Bharath all these years rather than constitution and the law.

Constitution was just ignored by not only the Congress party but also the entire opposition for their own reasons. All the popular leaders from across party lines were included in the ad hoc ministry of Nehru from 1947 to 1952. If anybody wants to contest as President in 1950, he had to first resign from the ministry. No minister took that chance.

Congress proposed Babu Rajendra Prasad and got him won. Nehru continued to play key role as Prime Minister without any constitutional authority while President remained an onlooker despite being bestowed with all the executive, judicial, administrative, financial, and military power of the state under Article 53. This lenience of Babu Rajendra Prasad towards Prime Minister Nehru, gave him opportunity to be President for two more terms.

If elections were held for the post of President in 1950, Sardar Vallabh Bhai Patel could be a strong contender against Nehru. Many princely states were merged with Bharath by resolute military action of Sardar Vallabh Bhai Patel, as Home Minister. States would have been gratuitous towards him for giving them state hood and democracy. Given the opportunity, they would exercise their first franchise in his favour for the post of President. Ambedkar too would have been another strong contender. Communists, Socialists, and others would anyhow field their own candidates. Who would have won could only be a guess.

The President, Babu Rajendra Prasad, was kept away from the party and politics. The superior has become subordinate and the subordinate has become superior to his master. Legislative and Executive Power got vested in the Prime Minister and the chief ministers unjustly against the constitution and against the cardinal principle of democracy, separation of Powers. Democracy was smashed in one stroke! Altogether a new model of governance was adopted by Nehru and accepted by the opposition parties as against what was contained in the Constitution.

# 7

# Servants are Ruling Against Their Master

People are carrying fads in their minds that the Prime Minister and Chief Ministers are people's men and hence that they are powerful while President is not so powerful being indirectly elected. The fact is other way round. Only President is elected while ministers are not.

P.V. Narasimha Rao was not member of any of the houses when sworn in as Prime Minister in 1991. Dr. Manmohan Singh was not an elected member of House of the People or the Council of States. Udhav Thackery, Mamata Banarjee, Yogi Adityanath, Nitish Kumar, Konijeti Roshaiah etc., past Chief Ministers were nominated MLCs. Appointed ministers, if not members of Assembly or council, have either to get elected or get nominated by Governor as members of the council, within six months of their appointment as ministers or as Chief Minister.

Since the term of office of Prime Minister is during the pleasure of the President under Article 75 (2) and the term of Chief Minister is during the pleasure of the Governor under Article 164 (2), a Prime Minister or Chief Minister cannot continue in office even for a moment without pleasure of the President or Governor which implies that their appointment shall also be at the pleasure of President or Governors.

Executive are members of the legislatures though not elected in terms of Articles 79 and 168. They need not attend the legislatures regularly. We know what happens in the Parliament and assemblies. Members call names each other, break the mikes and throw them at each other, tear off the bills and throw them on the face of the speaker, bash up each other with fists, rush to the podium berserk and create pandemonium necessitating their suspension and throwing out of the house physically by the marshals. President and Governors are not such authorities to sit in such atmosphere. Executive must be vigilant in administering the country instead of sitting in the legislatures and witnessing the pandemonium.

It sounds ridiculous to say that President and Governors hold all the Executive Power of the Union and of the states, but they should exercise it in accordance with advice of the council of ministers who are subordinate to them. Even a child can understand the falsity of this proposition. It means that President and Governors have no power whatsoever except following the advices of the council of ministers. This was contemplated by 42nd amendment of 1976 by Indira Gandhi to lend legality to the illegal practice adopted until then. Unfortunately, the President attested his seal and signature on this amendment. This amendment sought, in one stroke, to shift the whole executive power of the Executive to their subordinates. This amendment just obliterated the dividing line between the Legislature and the Executive which is an essential feature of democracy. In one word, it destroyed democracy altogether. This is not just a deviation; it is destruction of the constitution; it is not amending, it is vandalizing.

It is the first and foremost duty of the present Parliament to nullify 42^{nd} amendment, to the extent of this provision. Alternatively, the President can just ignore this amendment and act according to the constitution but, to do this, he should be dynamic. If the President assents to such bills which take away his rights and responsibilities as President, he is deemed to have violated the constitution, but such amendments shall not be valid. Now, it is the President who alone can erect Bharathiya sovereignty with his action or destroy it altogether with his inaction. He should be bold and decisive within the purview of the constitution. Constitution provided him so many safe guards. None can remove him or take any action against him unless he violated the constitution.

There are several Articles in the Constitution like Article 352 and 356, which postulate the opinion, satisfaction, belief, consider necessary, suitable, etc. words regarding discretionary powers of the President. When we say he has discretion, we cannot say simultaneously that he must act in accordance with advices of somebody. Discretion is different from obeying.

In fact, the whole constitution revolves around functions of the President of Bharath. References to Prime Minister or Chief Ministers are not found anywhere in the constitution except regarding their appointment, their right to choose members of council of ministers under Articles 75 and 164 and their responsibility to furnish information to President or the Governors under Articles 78 and 167.

If the Executive are required to act according to advices of council of ministers, how can they appoint ministers? It is illogical to think. Ministers do not exist before they are appointed by the Executive. It is funny to think that Prime Ministers and Chief Ministers should be dismissed at their own advice or on the advice of council of ministers.

President's oath of office is far reaching and has no boundaries. Only his ability is the limit to his power. The words "best of my ability" and "devote myself" contained in his oath suggest that he shall not spare any efforts to keep up his oath. He can travel even beyond the Constitution if it is required to protect the Constitution and the law and for securing the wellbeing of the people of Bharath.

Under Article 161, a state Governor shall act according to instructions of the President in matters not provided for in the constitution. It means that the President can use his discretion in matters not provided for in the constitution or when there is ambiguity. His ability cannot be limited to complying with the advice of ministers.

President may be elected with simple majority in the Electoral College but, his removal requires two thirds majority in both houses of Parliament separately. He cannot be impeached with whatever majority in both houses of Parliament, if he did not violate the constitution. The constitution intended that the country shall not go even for a single day without a President in place. In contingencies like his death, resignation or impeachment, the next incumbent would be elected as soon as possible within six months during which period, the Vice President would act as President.

Total population of a state, not voters, is divided by the number of Assembly constituencies in that state to arrive at the average vote value of an MLA in that state. For convenience, the value is expressed in thousands. The value of each elected member of Parliament i.e., other than nominated by the President, is derived by dividing the value of total votes of M.L.A.s in the country by the number of elected members of both houses of Parliament.

Votes of MLAs constitute 50% of Electoral College; Lok Sabha members constitute 35% and Rajya Sabha members, 15%. They are about 230, elected by the state Assembly members. Thus, the aggregate votes of assemblies and Council of States together would be 65% while that of the House of the People are only 35%. It shows the importance of state assemblies in electing the President who is the real sovereign power of this country.

In view of the above discussion, we should understand that President is deemed to have been elected by the people of Bharath. Otherwise, there is no purpose in counting popular votes along with electoral votes. This is also the method of election of President of America with some variation.

We have seen, House of the People has only 35% of votes in the Electoral College. Someone is becoming Prime Minister with majority in the House of the People which means he has support of 18% of total votes of the Electoral College through his own party or in coalition with other parties. If it is a coalition Prime Minister, as head of the single largest party in the coalition, he could be having about 9% of the votes of the Electoral College i.e., less than 10%. His existence would be dependent on the mercy of coalition parties which are not under his control. Any party or group of members may withdraw support to the coalition, leading to collapse of the marquee of the Prime Minister. This unconstitutional process leads to instability of governments and immorality in their formation and dissolution.

The minimum age limit to contest to Assembly or to House of the People is 25 years. It is 30 years in case of State Legislative Councils and the Council of States. For the President and Governors, the minimum age prescribed under Article 58 is 35. Under American constitution too, minimum age prescribed for members of House of Representatives is 25, for senators 30 and for President, it is 35. It indicates that a more mature, wisdom, restraint, dispensation, and diligence is expected of the President and Governors. It is not necessary for the President or the Governors to be older than all the members of the Parliament and assemblies if they are to act as secretaries.

President of Bharath is elected by majority of the Electoral College consisting of about 4000 M.L.A.s and 750 Parliament members. If someone elected as leader of a political party or a coalition by about a 50 M.L.A.s or 300 M.P.s get so much power as Chief Minister or Prime Minister, how powerful a President should be having been elected for 5-year term with his designation as President by thousands of M.L.A.s and M.P.s?

# 8

# Extensive Powers Of The President

Article 3 says, to alter states' names, areas, boundaries, status etc., bills shall not be introduced in the Parliament without recommendation of the President.

Art 53 says, executive power of union shall be vested in the President of Bharath. which he may exercise by himself directly or through officers subordinate to him. It does not mean that he shall not do anything without being advised by his subordinates.

Article 54 says that the President shall be elected by the Electoral College and Article 55 states that his election shall be done through secret ballot and 56 provides that the term of office of President shall be 5 years. Article 60 contains his oath of office and 61 explains the process of his impeachment.

Article 72 says, President has powers to remit punishments imposed by the Hon'ble Supreme Court. Art. 73 states that the executive power of President extends to whole territory of Bharath in matters regarding which the Parliament has right to make laws.

Article 74 and 75 state that the union council of ministers shall be appointed by the President to aid and advise him in exercising his duties and that their terms of office shall be during the pleasure of the President. Art. 76 empowers him to appoint and remove Attorney General to advise him on legal matters.

Art. 77 states that all executive actions of Bharathiya union shall be taken out in the name of the President. Art. 78 enjoins upon the Prime Minister, the duty to report to the President regarding all decisions of council of ministers regarding administration of the affairs of the union and proposals for legislation.

Under Art. 80, President can appoint 12 persons, who are experts in certain fields, to the Council of States. Under Art. 171, Governors can appoint $1/6^{th}$ of Members to the state Legislative Council, who are experts in certain fields.

Under Article 85, President has right to prorogue Parliament and dissolve Lok Sabha from time to time. Under Articles 86 and 87, President has right to summon and address both houses of Parliament together or separately. President has right to take oath of office from newly elected or nominated members of Parliament under Art. 99. Under Art. 103, President shall decide whether any member acquired any disqualifications prescribed by the constitution to continue as member.

We know, no bill becomes law until assented to by the President under Article 111. Under Art. 112, it is the President who should cause to introduce Annual Financial Statement in the Parliament every year. President is empowered under Art. 123, to issue ordnances during recess of Parliament.

The judges of The Supreme Court are appointed by the President and they are impeached with his signature after passing in Parliament under Art. 124. The change in location of the Supreme Court as decided by the Chief Justice, needs approval of President under Art. 136. President is entitled to seek advice of The Hon'ble Supreme Court under Art. 143. The President has right to appoint and transfer High Court judges under Art. 222. Comptroller and Auditor General of Bharath is appointed by the President under Art. 148. He is required to submit his annual report to the President under Art. 151 which will be placed before the Parliament by the President.

Governors have executive power of states under Art. 154. They are appointed by President to hold office during his pleasure under Art. 155 and 156. In terms of Art. 160, Governors shall act according to instructions of the President in matters where the constitution is not clear. In one word, to save repetition, all the rights and responsibilities of Governors in states under different Articles, are akin to those of the President at the union level. Under Art.

239, President administers Union Territories through administrators appointed by him for that purpose. Under Art. 274, President's permission is necessary to introduce bills which affect taxation in which states are interested.

President appoints Finance Commission under Article 280 every 5 years which recommends financial outlays and centre state distribution of funds. Custody of the union funds is regulated by the rules made by the President while custody of state funds is regulated by rules made by the Governor under Article 283. All government contracts and insurances are taken in the name of the President or the Governor under Art. 299 but, neither the President nor the Governors shall be personally held responsible under them.

Terms of all Bharath services like IAS, IPS, IRS, IFS etc. and other central defence services shall be during the pleasure of the President and terms of state services shall be during the pleasure of the Governors under Art. 310. Chairmen and members of union and state Public Service Commissions shall be appointed by the President and Governors respectively at their pleasure, under Art. 316. These Commissions are required to submit annual reports to President and Governors.

President appoints chairmen of National SC commission, ST commission and BC commission under Articles 338, 338A and 338B and he can amend the lists of castes following due process under

Art. 340, 341, 342 and 342A. President also appoints Parliamentary committee on official language under Art. 344 and he can appoint special officer under Art. 350B for linguistic minorities.

President is empowered to declare state of emergency under Art. 352 over all or any part of Bharath and he is also empowered to dissolve state assemblies when he opined that certain conditions existed under Art 356. He can also declare financial emergency under Art. 360. He is not answerable for his executive actions to courts under Art. 361. He can issue directions to states under Articles 256 and 257 and if they are not complied with, he may take it as breakdown of constitutional mechanism in the state under Article 365 and proceed to dissolve the concerned assemblies under Article 356. We know, no constitutional amendment under Article 368 becomes effective unless assented to by the President.

Under Article 364, notwithstanding anything in this Constitution, President may by public notification direct that as from such date as may be specified in the notification—

a. any law made by Parliament or by the Legislature of a State shall not apply to any major port or aerodrome or shall apply thereto subject to such exceptions or modifications as may be specified in the notification, or

b. any existing law shall cease to have effect in any major port or aerodrome except as respects things done or omitted to be done before the said date, or shall in its application to such port or aerodrome have effect subject to such exceptions or modifications as may be specified in the notification.

Thus, he has command over all Ports and Aerodromes, Armed Forces, Executive, Legislative, Judicial, Administrative and Financial functions of Bharath. It is misfortune of this country that such an elaborately elected and empowered President is treated as secretary to his own appointed subordinates.

Bharath, being huge in size and strength like an elephant, may not be brought down by a single blow, but is bound to succumb to incessant onslaught. In my opinion, Bharath is at the verge of disaster due to ignoring of its constitution and due to adopting of Pakistan constitution.

Through Kesavanada Bharathi case, the court propounded an abstract Basic Structure Theory under which it limited the power of Parliament and the President under Article 368 to amend the constitution. In fact, we should not replace the wisdom of 800 elected, responsible, answerable parliamentarians by knowledge of a few Supreme Court judges. In fact, basic structure of the constitution is "Sovereign Democratic Republic." Justice, Liberty, Equality are the purposes and Democracy is the process required for constituting India in to a Sovereign Democratic Republic. This structure is seminal to realizing all the objectives envisioned in the constitution. The expectations from the basic structure and the process of its construction should not be confused with the basic structure itself. Moreover, it is the duty of the President to protect the constitution; not of Judiciary who took oath to be truly abide by the constitution.

We should mull over as to why so many duties, discretions, rights, and responsibilities are enlisted for the President if he is required to blindly follow his subordinates namely, ministers? Instead, it could be provided that the President shall act in accordance with the advices of the council of ministers. To so happen for the last 75 years in a vast country like Bharath, is enormous misfortune of the people of this country.

In fact, President should be a politician and lead his party to success in the general elections so that he can solicit their vote in the Presidential elections. It is natural injustice to say that President should not have role in the election of his party candidates. How can he go and solicit their votes for his election? It would be like begging. Every thing, the party, the legislatures, the governments are left in the hands of concerned Prime Minister and Chief Ministers which made the President a nominal head of state. In fact, he should be the head of a political party and of the state.

# 9

# President Can, But May Not, Save The Country

If Parliament is filled with state or small parties, they may pass bill for bifurcation of the country in to 30 pieces so that each of them could become Prime Ministers to each of the fragment. Let us assume that they have sent the bill to the President who is under the wrong impression that he is bound to assent to any bill passed in the Parliament and to follow the advice of council of ministers.

Bharathiya people are already divided among themselves psychologically based on language, caste, region, religion and economic disparities while physical division is pending which is looming large. Division of the country takes place the next moment small and state parties, which are based on the divisive concepts enlisted above, together secure majority in both houses of Parliament. Politicians do not mind bifurcating the country in to any number of pieces if they could become Prime Minister of one of it.

By forming linguistic states, hatred started among people of Bharath based on language. We can see the examples of Tamil Nādu, Andhra, Telangana, Mumbai etc. Allowing small and state parties to come in to existence is like giving political license to an organization to lead movement for separation of the country, officially. People of different regions hate each other based on their place of birth or domicile.

If there were no small and state parties in the state of Jammu and Kashmir, there would have not been demand for plebiscite in that state or its merger with Pakistan or special rights to it. If there are only two parties in the country both of which are national, such things could never have happened in Kashmir.

Region and Religion are the two main factors which are potential enough for separation of country. It was only on this basis that Bharath and Pakistan were formed as separate countries. If polity joins the cause, division of the country becomes imminent. Successive governments have done little to resolve these conflicts after independence. Instead, they are playing with these factors indiscriminately to gain vote banks. Governments are discriminating people based on caste and religion for political gains.

Once Bharath is divided in to several small countries, its far and near aliens would capture state by state. China, Pakistan and Nepal are already claiming parts of Bharath as theirs and making all sorts of efforts to occupy them. There are still some countries who treat Bharath as an unclaimed territory and hence that they too have right to migrate in to it. Once they capture any one state of Bharath which emerged as a separate country due to division, it forms their base for invading other small countries of Bharath with help of other countries in the region. History repeats. This is exactly the way in which countries in this subcontinent fell to foreign invaders in the past.

Once, a country is lost to invaders, the invaders would not behave humane. There would be political holocaust, looting, arson, terror, rape and slavery with vengeance.

The British have consolidated and handed over the present vast Bharath to the Bharathiya leaders. It was an opportunity and a challenge for the Bharathiya leaders to administer a vast country with varied cultures and regions. They failed miserably in forging fraternity in the minds of the people as enunciated in the preamble of the constitution. They have not honed their skills as leaders. Instead, they kept playing the game of divide and rule, by inciting division of people on caste, region and religious lines, unconcerned about fraternity, unity and integrity of the country. These scandalous politics of Bharath can neither protect the sovereignty of the country nor can preserve the unity and integrity of the country nor can nurture nationality in the hearts of people nor can serve them for long.

The biggest national parties namely B.J.P., and Congress do not have majority in major assemblies in the country. Even the political capital of Bharathiya Union, Delhi and the financial capital, Mumbai are in the hands of the small and state parties. This is indicative of the situation to come. Both these parties should unite to politically unite the country or else, these two parties, one after the other, would be reduced to less than a regional party in terms of size in due course.

Let us examine a case where the Parliament being filled with dozens of small and state parties, passed a bill for bifurcation of the country in to thirty small countries and sent the bill to the President for his assent with an advisory letter from the council of ministers that the bill be assented by the President forthwith. Their idea could be to divide the country in to thirty pieces among them so that thirty of them could become Prime Ministers, 30 Presidents and hundreds of ministers.

Let us consider what The President should do on receipt of the bill for bifurcation of the country. In terms of the 42$^{nd}$ constitutional amendment of 1976, President has no other choice but to accede to the advice of council of ministers. If he assents to the bill, the country will be fragmented in to thirty pieces. All national institutions including the Supreme Court would get bifurcated along with territory of the country. Should it happen so easily at the whims and fancies of small and state parties? No, the Constitution does not allow such thing to happen.

Let us assume, the President sought the advice of the Supreme Court under Article 143, for which he is entitled, with query, whether he was bound to assent to the bill for bifurcation of the country or not. The

Supreme Court advises the President that the bill need not be assented to by him in view of the objective of "Unity and Integrity" contained in the Preamble and that the preamble is unalterable and that it should be respected at all cost. Accordingly, President withholds the bill citing the Preamble and the opinion of the Supreme Court.

Parliament members being angered with the advice of the Supreme Court against their resolution for bifurcation of the country, passed a resolution under Article 124 impeaching the Chief Justice of Bharath and other judges who gave that advice, and sent the bill to the President for his signature which is mandatory under that Article. If President signs the impeachment resolution, the judges are deemed impeached. It is insult to the President if the judges are impeached for giving him advice in accordance with the constitution and at his behest. Should the President allow the judges to be impeached for performing their Constitutional duty of advising him? If he allows, he loses his credibility as head of state. It is equivalent to losing his job.

He again seeks advice of the Supreme Court whether was he bound to sign the resolution impeaching the Supreme Court judges. The Supreme Court again advises the President that he need not and should not sign the impeachment resolution. It reminds him, it is he who should "Protect the constitution and the law" in accordance with his oath of office under Article 60. The President naturally refrains from signing the impeachment resolution even after being advised by the council of ministers and communicates his refusal to the Parliament.

Being further angered, Parliament moves resolution for the impeachment of the President himself under Article 61 which does not require his assent. President attends that house of the Parliament in which his impeachment is being discussed and advances his arguments against bifurcation of the country, for which he is entitled under Article 61 but, to no avail. The impeachment is passed following due process with two thirds majority in both houses of Parliament. The Parliament members start making arrangements for election of new President and for bifurcation of the country. Should the President relinquish his office as President because of his impeachment in the Parliament? No, if he does that, the Supreme Court also would get dissolved and the country gets bifurcated. Our Constitution is a robust piece of enactment which has provided for all sorts of contingencies. It does not allow the country to be divided.

The President again seeks advice of The Court regarding Constitutionality of his impeachment. The court advises him that the impeachment is invalid under Article 61 because the President has not violated the Constitution; in fact, he tried to protect it. The court brings to the notice of the President of his oath of office under Article 60 to "Preserve, Protect and Defend the Constitution and the law to the best of his ability and to devote himself for the service and wellbeing of the people of Bharath" and advises him to protect the constitution, law, unity and integrity of the nation. President communicated the advice of the Court to the Parliament and refused to relinquish his office as President. The Parliament members just tore off orders of the court and of the President and went ahead with their plans for bifurcating the country.

Then the President would show his ultimate power as head of state. He would dismiss all union ministers under Article 75 and all the Governors and assemblies of states under Article 156 and 356. He will clamp emergency throughout the country under Article 352 and if necessary, deploys armed forces of which he is the supreme commander. We should also not forget that the state courts are subordinates to Supreme Court while States Governors, I.A.S. and I.P.S. and other central and state services employees are subordinates to the President and not to the ministers. They are the employees of the government represented by President and Governors. They follow the orders of the President but not of ministers, state or central.

It is only the President who can save the country, Constitution and the law and none other under the constitution. The law and order of the country is reposed in the President. Law is represented by the hierarchy of courts in Bharath and order is represented by the civil staff, police and three armed forces of the country. The secessionist leaders would not be able to wag their tails anymore. If any constituency leader tries to play smart, he can get imprisoned by the President. If President becomes a dictator, the people and the opposition leaders would revolt.

Supposing the President is also offered one piece of the divided country, he may not so be tempted because he is already the ruler of a large and undivided Bharath, if he feels, he is the real head of the state. However, it is possible for the President to yield to gratifications in the present format in which he is only a symbolic head of state, without any real powers to him. If the President of Bharath is holding real power as given to him by the constitution, as head of Bharathiya Union or Bharathiya Republic, he would never yield to such gratifications and hence, Bharath would never get bifurcated. He may get tempted in the present form of Presidential status because he may consider it better to be head of a dog than being tail of a lion. As such, the need of the hour is to restore all the powers of the President to him forthwith.

If unitary and republic form of governance is adopted as presented in the constitution, Bharath will be a heaven for its inhabitants to live with peace, prosperity and individual dignity instead of it being a haven for illicit political brewing as of today. There may be operational problems here and there in establishing a unitary and republic government in Bharath. The need is to remove the obstacles through constitutional amendments which may be made to realize the objectives of the constitution instead of amending the objectives. Constitution is already amended 104 times and making of one more amendment should not be a problem.

# 10

# Multiparty System Is Not True Democracy

If hundreds of people contest for the same Assembly or Parliament segment, theoretically, somebody can win even with less than 1% of polled and valid votes. It is not democracy: it is hypocrisy or self-deceit.

Under multiparty system, people are not sure of any party forming government. One party becomes the largest or the single largest party while some other party forms government in coalition with some other small and sundry parties of diverse objectives. Governments move without direction. People lose interest in voting because their vote may not count. Will of people is demonstrated stronger only under bi-party system.

53 political parties contested in the first general elections of 1952, but people have made their opinion known by giving 45% votes to Congress party and 55% to all the opposition parties put together. People considered the politics as Congress versus non-Congress. Opposition parties were in plenty and they solicited votes on several grounds such as region,

religion, language, caste, communism, and liberalism and hence, probably got 55% of votes in aggregate. If they were united in to one party and fought election under one leadership and on one slogan, they and Congress could have got almost equal percentage of votes and one of them would have won with slender majority which would have meant a healthy democracy for the country.

Representation of people Act was made in hurry and when there was no regular parliament which came in to existence in 1952 after the First general elections. After the elections, there would be elected representatives of the people and a government in place and a venue called Parliament to debate and decide on the subject. Based on people's opinion and that of the elected representatives, the government that emerged after the first elections should have taken a call on the system of polity for the country, whether to have a two-party system or multiparty system or some other system to obtain opinion of 51% of the public.

Having no political parties at all or having multiple political parties in the elections would not serve the purpose of democracy and hence, inevitable option is only two-party system. Since the constitution did not have mention of political parties in it, we cannot deduce that the Constitution intended a no party system for Bharath. In a no-party system, any citizen who possessed the qualifications and who is not subjected to any disqualifications under the constitution, could contest elections. He would not be bound by any party discipline. It would be worse than multi-party system since several members could contest for the same constituency.

Inviting the single largest party leader to form government, head count of legislators to prove majority, party defections, breakaway groups, party mergers, party coalitions, issuing of whips, no confidence motions on the floor of the house etc. were not provided under the constitution because the aforesaid mal practices were not required under a two-party system.

In one-word, Bharathiya political system has become a mockery of the constitution and a foul play. Elections and politics have become bread and butter for the people and for the political parties as well. Bharathiya political system serves an example for other countries to understand how not to run their countries.

We can also see what is happening in Kashmir. The same thing could not have happened if there were no small and state parties in that state and there were only two national political parties in that state. None of the two parties would have supported plebiscite in Kashmir or separate status for it or acceding it to Pakistan. No national party would espouse the cause of secessionist forces based on religion, caste, or region lest it should lose credibility in other regions. If there are only two political parties, none of them can behave without responsibility.

We are also witnessing short lived governments at the centre and states due to multiparty coalitions, defections, mid-term elections and multiple elections in different states. In fact, they are not governments; they are power monger gangs formed to exploit state resources. What they are indulging in is not politics except a foul play.

We have also been witnessing secessionist movements and conflicts of caste, region and religion and cross boarder terrorism in several states right from the beginning. Yet, our leaders have not woken up to the situation. Instead, they are using the differences among people as political weapons to gain vote banks.

Political zamindari families have dawned due to multiparty system in various parts of the country, claiming rights over regions. The situation that existed before far-flung regions of Bharathiya sub-continent lost to invaders is being recreated. Innumerable small and state parties mushroomed all over the country, registered under the Representation of People Act 1951. National parties are slowly losing their hold on states while small and state parties in the states are vying with each other to establish their hold over the states.

The social, political, and financial profits of establishing political parties, to the high commands, their families, friends, and relatives, are manifold and enormous. They could become kings or king makers depending on their luck. We can imagine how powerful these party high commands could be, having so many rich and influential followers expecting tickets and contract works and other government permissions and positions. Party high commands could pass on their positions to their heirs by heredity.

We witnessed frequent shifting of loyalties by leaders form one party to the other. Leaders do not shift loyalties from one party to the other if there were only two parties in the country because neither party dies down. Each of the parties will be either in power or in opposition. Leaders nurture hope of coming to power at some time or the other in future.

To infuse stability in to polity of the country and to arrest political immorality it is a must to shift to two-party system forth with. The process, at present, is made complicated due to presence of strong regional party system but, it is inevitable to dissolve all of them in to one of the two parties if you want to save sovereignty, unity, and integrity of the country. When they can function under two main coalitions, why should they not merge in to one party?

One of my senior advocate friends argued that it was fundamental right of citizens to form associations. True, they can register as voluntary service organizations, devotional or cultural organizations or trade Unions or co-operative societies. There are separate enactments for that purpose under the state and central lists as well. They need not register under the Representation of People Act as political parties. It is a specific enactment to register only political parties. Neither service organizations can be registered under this Act, nor political parties can be registered under Registration of Societies Acts, state or central.

One may also argue that it is fundamental right of citizens to propagate their ideals and beliefs. Even then it is not necessary to register a political party and contest elections. Political parties are formed essentially to gain power and to run the governments with authority. They cannot be equated with voluntary service organizations. More number of service organizations may be good for the society but multiple political parties are not good for the country.

If multiple small and sundry parties have opportunity to decide who should be the President or Prime Minister of Bharath, they would always choose such person who would not interfere with their corruption.

# 11

# Political Fronts Are Illegal

Political fronts are illegal since they are not registered or registerable under the Representation of the People Act or any other enactment. There is neither mention of political fronts in the Constitution nor does any law recognize them. Only individual citizens can form political parties under Representation of People Act 1951. It defined political party as "An association of individual citizens of Bharath, registered as political party under Section 29A of that Act". The irony is that, the political coalitions being illegal, are playing an important role in making and breaking of governments and in making of laws for the country.

Due to germination of innumerable political parties, a stock market like situation has arisen in Bharathiya politics. Nobody knows which party makes pre pole and post pole adjustment with which party and why. Nobody knows when and why they unite or they break up. Nobody knows which party joins alliance and which party supports government from outside and why and how long. These political coalitions are not based on moral or ideological thinking. This opportunistic behaviour of politicians, unfortunately, is being praised as political acumen, political astuteness and so on.

One of the best and the recent example of distortion of public opinion through political coalitions is Karnataka. BJP and Congress got near 100 seats each in 2018 elections. Congress and BJP wanted to prevent each other from forming of government. In this process, Congress party supported Kumara Swamy led Janata Dal ( Secular ) who had only 25 seats whereby he became the Chief Minister, but it was not the intention of the people of Karnataka. We cannot say, it is a popular government as mentioned in S.R. Bommai case.

Coalitions are opportunistic arrangements for sharing political power. Coalition partners go to the extent of bringing down the coalition government if they do not get the expected ministries in the government, especially the post of Prime Minister and Chief Minister. This was what Janata coalition did in 1980 and U.P.A in 1998.

We witnessed several Indian Prime Ministers and states Chief Ministers visiting foreign countries and the United Nations and representing Bharath and addressed such august gatherings. They were acclaimed for their eloquent speeches and ideals. However, they faced no confidence motions immediately on their return to Bharath. Thus, their positions in the present lopsided system are fragile and our leaders become laughing stock for other countries.

Bharath would be divided into several pieces no sooner than coalitions of small and sundry parties muster two-thirds majority in both houses of Parliament. No force can stop it in view of the 42$^{nd}$ constitutional amendment to the affect that the President shall act only in accordance with the advice of the council of ministers and that he shall not withhold his assent for the bills passed in the Parliament.

Some of my friends argued that there was military to protect integrity of the country in such eventuality. But who will command the army. It is the President who should do that, but the President and the Prime Minister who belong to a coalition of parties may not be interested in that. If the army does it on its own, it would be still worse which will be end of democracy.

Supporting of governments from outside, without joining them, is another Constitutional atrocity. We know the cost of carrying the coalition governments by the outside parties on their heads. The outside supporting parties enjoy better privileges, than the ruling coalition partners, without any responsibility. They withdraw their support to the coalition government just before elections on some pretext or the other lest their distinct entity as political party should get eroded in the minds of voters. Of course, they join the coalition again after elections, on one pretext or the other. Government runs on mercy of coalition partners, sometimes, on mercy of a single coalition partner. It leads to political instability, immorality, and blackmailing.

Majority of political parties in Assembly or House of the People is liable to be changed any time and any number of times during the term of the house. Opposition party becomes ruling party and opposition leader becomes Chief Minister overnight due to defections. Getting two members from the ruling side is sufficient to turn the tables. This malpractice of reckoning majority in a house for the purpose of determining the Prime Minister or Chief Minister instils instability in to the governance and immorality in to the polity of the country.

# 12

# Linguistic, Unequal States Are Sown Weeds

In Bharath, states were formed in the past and are being re-organized in the present in violation of Articles 55, 80, 81, 170 and 368. Governments are so doing by citing Article 3 which is only an enabling provision which is not complete in itself. One must see Articles 55, 80, 81, 170 and 368 for the procedures and principles to follow in forming different states.

Article 55 states that each state shall have, as far as practicable, equal representation in the election of the President. This is important because, the President should give equal importance to all the states as Executive Power of Union. If some states are big like Uttar Pradesh and some others are small like Himachal Pradesh, he gives importance to bigger states because, he gets more votes in those states. In this process, small states get neglected and would not get the development they need.

Article 81 (2) reads, "For the purposes of subclause (a) of clause (1),

    a. there shall be allotted to each State a number of seats in the House of the People in such manner that the ratio between that number and the population of the State is, so far as practicable, the same for all States; and

b. each State shall be divided into territorial constituencies in such manner that the ratio between the population of each constituency and the number of seats allotted to it is, so far as practicable, the same throughout the State:

Provided that the provisions of sub-clause (a) of this clause shall not be applicable for the purpose of allotment of seats in the House of the People to any State so long as the population of that State does not exceed six million. This proviso was incorporated in 1973 after linguistic states were already organized in 1956 while ignoring the constitution.

Article 170 (1). Subject to the provisions of article 333, the Legislative Assembly of each State shall consist of not more than five hundred, and not less than sixty, members chosen by direct election from territorial constituencies in the State.

Article 170 (2) "For the purposes of clause (1), each State shall be divided into territorial constituencies in such manner that the ratio between the population of each constituency and the number of seats allotted to it shall, so far as practicable, be the same throughout the State.

We know vote value of state legislators is equivalent to the average population of an Assembly constituency in a state. The basis of assigning of value to votes of the Parliament Members is the average value of votes of MLAs in the country. The value of each vote of an M.L.A. is equivalent to the value arrived at by dividing the total population of that state by the total number of the M.L.A.s in that state.

When we say that each state, as far as practicable, shall have equal representation in the election of the President, it means that each state shall have equal number of populations, equal number of M.L.A.s and equal number of M.P.s. Otherwise, the vote value of M.L.A.s of each state and total value of each state would vary. It means that states should be formed based on population; not on political, linguistic, regional or other reasons. This has never been followed in Bharath.

Article 170 states each state shall have Assembly constituencies ranging from 60 to 500. It does not mean that some states can have 60 and some other, 500. If it is interpreted that way, Article 55 becomes meaningless and the equality of states in the Presidential elections get seriously affected. If there is more population and a smaller number of Assembly constituencies in a state, the value of vote of each MLA would be more in comparison with other states and the President would concentrate more on votes of MLAs of that state. To obviate such an eventuality, all states should have as far as practicable, equal population, equal number of Assembly constituencies and equal number of Lok Sabha seats and equal number of Rajya Sabha seats.

In terms of Article 368, any amendment resulting in change in conditions of Articles 54 and 55 shall have to be ratified by half of assemblies in the country. This vindicates the importance of equal representation given to the states in the Presidential elections. This provision is totally ignored by the country ever since beginning in forming and reorganization of states. So much of importance is accorded to formation of states by the constitution because they are crucial in electing the President who is Executive Power of this country.

It is imperative to reorganize all the states in Bharath, now, based on population, to make all of them equal as far as practicable. Congress party kept the U.P. as the biggest state and successive members from Nehru family contested to Lok Sabha from this state to own it which has now become a curse for that party. It went in to the hands of S.P., B.S.P., and the B.J.P.

Constitution prohibited discrimination of citizens based on region, religion and language. Hence, organization of linguistic states was also unconstitutional. Due to such reorganization of states, some states have become too big and some have become too small. If states are organized based on population, each state would have in it, people speaking more than one language whereby Hindi, as link language would have flourished as contained in the Directive Principles of State Policy of the constitution.

We are seeing linguistic and regional conflicts in several states which even went up to demanding to sever them from Bharath to form their own country. Such movements in the past, in Kashmir, Punjab, Nagaland etc., several states were militant and hence could be subdued with military force. Now, due to formation of small parties, such parties can get the bill for bifurcation of the country passed in the Parliament if their coalitions have majority in both houses of Parliament. Even if they do not have majority in the Parliament, they can officially demand in the Parliament for bifurcation of the country and encourage their political leaders and cadre in the states to organize mass movements. This paves way to bifurcation of the country.

# 13

# Freebies and Notes To Votes Are Like Narcotics

Political parties tend to promise all frees to woo voters, in greed to come to power at the centre or in the state, lured by the post of Prime Minister and Chief Minister which offer them unlimited power like that of a monarch. These inducements could include distribution of pensions, provisions and privileges to some specified sections of people, distribution of articles like mixers, grinders, motor vehicles and electrical and electronic gadgets. This is brazen show of disparity among citizens with authority and without responsibility.

National parties can not resort to such practices because of their presence in several states where the social and financial conditions are different. Small and state parties can announce schemes specific to their states. For this purpose, governments may be tempted to raise taxes, loans and sell government properties. Instead of developing the state with own resources, raw-materials, entrepreneurs and manpower, they invite foreign corporates to establish their industries in their state by providing state's resources to them at thrown away prices and show these industries and infrastructure as development they achieved. Declaring of different welfare schemes in different states defies equality of status and of opportunity among people of different states. It defies equality of opportunity among political parties in the elections.

This practice is against Article 14 of the constitution. In the Assembly elections, ruling party or its main opposition party could promise to distribute public money to specified people in their manifestos after their coming to power. Such opportunity is not available for independent contestants or small and marginal political parties in the state because it would be more fun than anything else if such small parties or independents make such poll promises as, "After coming to power." Equality among the contestants in elections is missing and hence, such poll promises or manifestos are unconstitutional being violative of Article 14.

Such poll promises or manifestoes are not only violative of Article 14, but are also illegal and unlawful being electoral offences. It is illegal either to pay or promise to pay money or money's worth to woo the voters through election manifestos. Such promises come under definition of Consideration, in terms of S. 2 (d) of Bharathiya Contract Act 1872. Hence, any promise contained in an election manifesto of any political party to the effect of promising any specified section of people, with specified amount of money or its worth, in consideration of voting it to power, is illegal, unlawful and an electoral offence. Political parties, in their election manifestos, may announce their priorities as to agriculture, social welfare, poverty alleviation, industrialization, national and international trade and industry, law and order etc. generally but they should not announce specific benefits to specific sections of voters while soliciting votes.

Under Article 112, it is the President who prepares the Annual Financial Statement which contains all the incomes and expenditures of the Union and he presents it before the House of the People for its consideration. The house of the People, under Article 113, New demands for expenditure cannot be put forth before the House without permission of the President. President is the custodian of the consolidated Fund of Bharath and every financial transaction of the union requires his assent. The relationship between a state Assembly and the Governor, regarding Annual Financial Statement of the state and Consolidated Fund of the state, is the same as that of President and the House of the People. Thus, electoral promises being made by the Prime Ministers and Chief Ministers on the election daises are unconstitutional and irregular.

Such unbridled poll promises, if unchecked, will bankrupt the country, create inequalities among people, destroy fraternity among citizens and would finally lead loss of fraternity and to bifurcation of the country. If social welfare schemes are permitted by the President and the Governors and passed in the Parliament and assemblies, the courts cannot and need not interfere under Articles 122 and 212, but if such manifestos are declared by political parties, outside the houses, they are illegal and the Election Commissions and the Courts can take actions including cancellation of election results Suo motto or on complaint.

If social welfare schemes are passed in the assemblies or Parliament, People can claim the benefits of such enactments as of right and the successive governments would not be able to change them without again passing the same in the Parliament or the Assembly. The ruling party would not be able to name these welfare schemes after their party leaders, parents, friends and relatives since they would be thoroughly discussed in the Assembly before passing them. The opposition parties also could play their role in passing such welfare schemes. It is after all the money of the government that is sought to be distributed through such schemes, rather than money of the ruling party or of individual leaders. Opposition parties would not oppose public welfare schemes. They, rather demand for more.

To arrest this, there is urgent need to adopt Unitary and Republic form of governance as prescribed by the constitution which can obviate centre state conflicts, promote nationalism and uniformity of administration throughout the country. Party owners would not spend crores of Rupees to win elections; they would not undertake tour on foot of hundreds of Kilo meters.

We cannot find fault with the people for accepting notes to votes. They are like water. Water flows in whatever way possible for it to move, due to gravity. Weakness or strength but it is the inherent characteristic of water. You cannot find fault with the water for its course. If you construct dams and canals and direct the water towards agricultural fields, it yields food for the people and provides waterways. If you let it lose, it can cause floods, inundate fields, and cause loss of life and havoc. So are people. They go to any extent to fill stomachs of themselves and their children, and justified.

Due to poverty, lacks of people are committing suicides, selling their kidneys and wombs. We cannot expect them to refuse notes for votes in elections. If you engage them in productive work, they bring peace and prosperity to the country. If they are let to go vagabond, they become threat to the society or become burden on it. It is not fault of the water or the people. It is fault of the leaders who are supposed to lead the water or the people for a productive purpose.

One may say, middle class and above middle class are also expecting rather than accepting notes for votes. True, they expect, accept or even demand notes for votes from the contestants because they know that the notes which are being distributed by the politicians are ill gotten and that the leaders, after winning the elections, will make much more money through corrupt practices.

The increasing cost of elections due to notes for votes has aggravated the situation. The leaders who have morals would be forced to leave politics being unable to face the new and usurping politicians who spend crores of Rupees in the elections. This works like Gresham's law in economics which states "Bad money drives out good money from the market." Genuine leaders would disappear while usurpers surface.

If people lose faith in democracy and judiciary, it leads to anarchy. Both of these institutions, at present, are on the verge of waning. Despite pecuniary inducements and sectoral incitements in the elections, the poll percentage on an average is not more than 70% across the country in Assembly or Parliament elections. If these illegal inducements are not offered by the contesting candidates to people, the poll percentage may be lower than 20%. It vindicates that the citizens do not nurture much faith in the present electoral process.

# 14

# Violation, Self Immolation Of Political Parties

All the political parties in Bharath suffered due to unconstitutional practices adopted in the country right from the beginning.

If two party system were adopted since independence, Congress party would have been either in power or in opposition till date, either of which positions is equally respectable. Several other political parties too disappeared from the political screen during the last 75 years. Several leaders of those extinct political parties might have lost money and mental peace.

Had the Unitary and Republican form of governance been adopted, most of the terms till day, members of Congress party would have been Presidents of Bharath because it was that party which had more of national faces that became prominent during the freedom struggle than any others.

If Regional Party System were not there, Rajiv Gandhi could have not been killed in Tamil Nadu in 1991 during his election campaign which did not have any effect on the elections. If there were only Two political parties in Bharath and if he were in power, his security would have been much stringent. Even if he were the sole opposition leader, his security would have been the responsibility of the ruling party. In either case, he could have not been killed so easily.

If secularism was not adopted, Indira Gandhi would not have sent troops in to the Golden Temple in Amritsar which resulted in her assassination by her own Sikh body guards in 1984 for sacrilege of their religious faith. Thought, expression, faith, belief and worship are the constitutional objectives. She ought not to have transgressed their religious faith. Due to pseudo secularism followed by the then governments, there has been hatred among different sections of the citizens leading to loss of fraternity.

Had the congress party not formed linguistic states, several states would have not been against the centre and the link language. Now, the linguistic states have become invincible for the national parties due to language barrier for the national leaders. It also resulted in people clashing among themselves in different states in the name of language.

Had the congress not formed inequal states, it would have not suffered political setbacks as it had. Congress party having bifurcated the country in to several states in the name of linguistic states, kept Uttar Pradesh as the largest against Article 55 purposefully.

All these incidents were irreparable loss not only to the Congress party but also to the whole nation. Congress party got benefited more out of mistakes of its opponents than out of its own strategies.

Opposition was divided in to several fragments and remained weak which became the strength of Congress party. Opposition leaders found it convenient and economical to establish small and state level parties and to form coalitions.

Ambedkar launched his own political party by name "Scheduled Castes Federation," in 1952, which was a strategic error. How other castes would vote that party if it was named after a particular caste? How he could win elections with Scheduled Caste votes alone? It resulted in defeat of himself and his party in the first general elections. The overwhelming majority of Congress party and utter failure of all others at the hustings made everybody dumbfounded. I am surprised how the constitutional drafting committee chairman registered his political party with name of a caste against constitutional philosophy of non-discrimination based on caste etc.

Communists being political party, were eager in condemning the faiths, beliefs and worships of people. They did not realize that finer feelings of faith and belief of people were nurtured with passion by people for centuries by succession which they consider as more valuable than their own lives. Bharath is a land of faiths whether it be Hindu, Christian, Muslim or other and people are forgiving. Communists advocated revolutionary and violent methods to bring about social, political and economic changes in the country. Bharathiya people are followers of Dharma and Karma and are influenced by the preaching and practices of various religious seers and Mahatma Gandhi, who did not endorse violence. All these communist groups and parties have the common objective of establishing communism in Bharath but varied only in the methods of achieving communism and degrees of violence.

# 15

# Dissolution Of Houses Midterm, A Sin

Dissolution of elected houses midterm is suicidal to democracy through self- immolation. It is like setting the house on fire to get rid of mice in it. It is the worst sort of crime against democracy.

At present, assemblies are being dismissed by the President, to hold elections afresh, on the advice of chief ministers to the Governors. House of the People are being dismissed by the President, to hold elections afresh, on the advice of Prime ministers which is an unconstitutional practice in Bharath.

Legislative and the Executive wings are different from each other. Governments are represented by the Executive i.e., President, Governors, ministers and government employees. Legislative is represented by the Parliament and the state Assemblies and Legislative Councils. Executive may or may not hold majority in the houses. In fact, it presents a healthy democracy only if Executive do not have majority in legislatures. Legislatures make law and the Executive rules the country in accordance with the law. Bills passed by the legislatures are checked and assented to by the Executive while the legislatures impeach the Executive if he violates the constitution. One controls the other and finally, people judge both of them in the next elections. This is the process of democracy enshrined in the constitution.

Executive should not dismiss the Legislative. Neither the Legislative should impeach the Executive at its whims and fancies. Bharathiyas understood neither their constitution nor democracy.

Union Councils of ministers are essentially appointed subordinates to the President. The state Council of Ministers are appointed subordinates to the Governors. At present, Prime Minister and Chief Ministers are getting those positions as of right due to their majority in the Lok Sabha or an assembly. It is not only unconstitutional, but also a dangerous dictatorial practice.

Midterm dissolution of Lok Sabha, based on advice of Prime Minister and midterm dissolution of assemblies based on advice of Chief Ministers and conducting of midterm elections to them, is prescribed under Articles 58 and 112 of the Pakistan Constitution, but not under any provisions of the Bharathiya constitution. Dissolving elected houses and conducting midterm elections to them is a sacrilege against democracy and the constitution. It is a dictatorial tendency. Unfortunately, unquestioningly, it was done several times in the past in the states and at the centre as well. The constitution has not provided for such a heinous act.

We should also remember that Prime Minister and chief Minister may or may not be elected members of House of the People or of a state Assembly. How, they being non-elected members of the houses, can advise for dissolution of the houses.

If a Prime Minister or a Chief Minister wants, they may resign their membership to the house, if they were members at all. All their followers, if any, may also resign and go for byelections for their seats. The President and Governors appoint another set of ministers and run the administration.

The houses continue to function as long they have minimum quorum under Articles 100 and 189, irrespective of vacancies in the houses. It is not an impediment in conducting of the houses or administering the country or the states with minimum quorum in houses. Otherwise, what is the purpose of prescribing minimum quorum to houses?

At present, members of assemblies and House of people, on declaring of dissolution of houses of which they are part, are running home like kids in schools, on declaring holidays to schools, with ecstasy. Should they not stand up and question "Why our memberships of house are cancelled midterm though we did not acquire any disqualifications prescribed under Article 102 or 191? We got elected by people for five years term under Article 83 or

172. We are not members of this house, at the mercy of the Prime Minister or the Chief Minister. Who is cancelling our memberships and why? Do they have authority to do so? If they have, under which provision of the constitution?" The question is, how these funny people who cannot protect their own constitutional rights as legislators, can protect the rights of people.

Article 352 is meant for imposing of emergency when safety of the country is at stake due to external aggression or internal disturbance. It is not meant for conducting of midterm elections. In fact, though emergency is declared by the President, it continues to be in force with concurrence of the Parliament every six months.

It is also vindicated by the language of Article 355 when it says that it is the responsibility of the union to deal with internal disturbances in a state. If necessary, the union would invoke Article 352. The Janata government with immaturity amended Article 352, through 43rd amendment of 1977, to exclude internal disturbances as cause for declaring emergency.

Article 356 is meant to deal with political disturbances in the states. It is the President who dissolves an assembly under Article 356 if he comes to the conclusion, based on the report of the Governor or otherwise, that administration of the state cannot be run in accordance with the provisions of the constitution. Mere Chief Minister's advice to the Governor is not sufficient for that purpose.

Political reasons under Article 356 include, when the opposition parties being in majority in the assembly, would not allow the Governor to summon them, address them or if they do not pass any bills including finance bills which are necessary to run the state or if they do not allow the legislatures to function in a normal way. Purpose of Article 356 is to deal with political disturbance in states while purpose of Article 352 is to deal with law-and-order situation in any part or whole of the country. Neither of these two articles are meant for conducting of midterm elections.

There is no reason as to why there should be midterm elections to any house. People have not committed any wrong in electing these members, nor did the members acquire any disqualifications. There can be re-elections if the process of elections is found to be illegal.

Advice by Prime Minister to the President to dissolve House of the People midterm is like advice to President to commit political suicide by him because he may lose his job after the midterm elections, if opposition parties gain majority in them. President becomes liable for impeachment because dissolving the House of the People midterm is an act of violation of Article 83 and 85 of the Constitution. Right given to President under Article 85 is to prorogue or dissolve the House of the People "From time to time" and not as and when he wished or the Prime Minister wished. From "time to time" means at the end of each term of five years.

The words "unless dissolved earlier" occurring in Articles 83 and 172 mean that the term of Lok Sabha or an Assembly could be less than Five years if declarations under Articles 352 or 356 were in operation by the end of term of Five years. For example, an Assembly is dissolved by the President under Article 356 about, say, one year before the end of Five-year term of the Assembly, then the term of the Assembly would be Four years. This is the true purport of Articles 83, 85, 172 and 174. However, elections should be held only after completion of term of Five years, or within 6 months thereafter under Article 352, but not midterm.

We witness opposition parties challenging the Prime Minister or a Chief Minister to dissolve the house midterm and go for midterm elections, if he has guts. Sometimes, Prime Ministers and Chief Ministers challenge or threaten to dismiss the houses and go for midterm elections. It is sheer ignorance, abysmal at that.

The House of the People was dissolved in 1971 because Congress did not have clear majority in both houses of Parliament due to split in it. Some of the bills like abolition of privy purses and nationalization of banks, proposed by Congress led government were defeated by single vote or were required to be passed with support of some consenting opposition parties. Congress party, annoyed with the situation, dissolved the House of the People midterm, and went for midterm poll in which it triumphed with 352 seats which is a different matter. Nevertheless, dissolution of House of People remains unconstitutional.

The opposition parties do not object to this evil practice because it would be another opportunity for them, to try their luck. There will again be pre-poll adjustments, post poll coalitions, underhand dealings and collection of funds. Elections are like festivals in Bharath for the voters and the leaders as well. Thus, ignorance, opportunities and conveniences ruled the roost and not the constitution and the law for the last 70 years in Bharath, ironically, in the name of the constitution.

State assemblies should survive their fixed term of five years under Article 172. Under Article 356, state assemblies are dissolved or suspended for a maximum period of three years. It is not necessary, proper or legal to conduct midterm elections during this period. The word "Dissolved," in relation to elected houses, is used in the constitution to mean "Suspended." Dissolution and suspensions are synonyms while Dissolution and dismissal are not. We can understand this through the procedures prescribed post dissolution of Assembly such as its review by Parliament from time to time and the maximum time limit of three years to keep an Assembly dissolved.

Under 356(2), the declaration made under Article 356 may be varied or rescinded by the President any time, at his option. If dissolution of assemblies is a permanent affair, time limit of three years and its review from time to time by parliament would have not been prescribed.

When an Assembly is dissolved, the functions of Assembly are discharged by the Parliament or its assigns while the government is taken over by the President or his assigns. They must be restored when the conditions have improved in the state. The same way emergency too should be recalled and the Lok Sabha restored once things improved in the country.

Hon'ble Supreme Court in S.R.Bommai case of 1994, observed that use of Article 356 is necessary in a country like India where there may be class and other conflicts. That is not a correct observation. To quell violence, state police is sufficient. If not, centre may deploy its forces under Article 355. If situation is still out of hands, Article 352 may be applied. 356 is not meant to deal with law-and-order situations. It is applicable to political situations which defy administration of the state in accordance with the provisions of the constitution. If there is failure of law and order, it is the failure of the Executive, not of legislatures. Why to dismiss legislatures and conduct midterm elections to them?

House of the People cannot be dissolved or suspended like an Assembly. There is also no provision in the constitution for dismissal of the House of the People. If House of the People is dismissed, there is no higher forum to look after its affairs. Even if a member or all its members resign, there will be bye elections to the vacancies but not midterm elections to the whole of the house.

There may be byelections to a seat or seats in House of the People or an Assembly, due to death, resignation or disqualification of members but midterm elections to the whole house is illegal. If they are really midterm elections, the houses that are formed after midterm elections should survive only for the rest of their original term. They cannot survive for another and fresh term of five years after midterm elections. Members and Governments may come and go midterm but the houses go on for their fixed term of five years.

Byelections are mentioned under Sections 149 and 150 of the Representation of People Act which we need not object to them. Though S. 14 and 15 of that Act alludes at midterm elections, they cannot be constitutionally valid without there being provision for midterm dismissal of elected houses or midterm elections in the constitution.

The quorum for meetings of state legislatures is 10% of total membership or 10 numbers whichever is higher under Article 189. If the opposition comprises more than 90% of an Assembly and yet, co- operates in conducting of the houses, and in passing of the bills, the Assembly need not be dissolved. Usually, the opposition party co-operates with the government to conduct the houses because it is routine occurrence under republic form of governance. The opposition utilizes the house to criticize the government.

Opposition members would never want the Assembly to be dissolved because they lose their opportunity to act as opposition.

S. 8 of the Representation of People Act 1951 and 10th Schedule to the constitution too are unconstitutional. Articles 102 and 191 prescribe conditions of disqualification and mentions that any additional disqualifications may be further added by Acts of Parliament. The prescribed disqualifications under these two Articles are natural reasons such as resignation, death, insolvency and disease. We should understand that further disqualifications which may be added through laws of parliament should be homogenous with the existing disqualifications.

For any personal offence committed by a member of the legislatures, he may be punished individually. For his personal crimes, people cannot be divested of their right to be represented. The punishment results in inequal treatment among M.L.Cs. M.L.As. R.S. members and Lok Sabha Members. Parliament membership is more valuable than the M.L.Cs. S. 8 of R.P. Act prescribes minimum of 2 years imprisonment as disqualification. Thus, a member can involve in several crimes which attract imprisonment for less than two years. It is not any wise enactment. Any member indicted in crime may be imprisoned, but he or she should be brought to the parliament or an assembly with police escort for participating in the proceedings of the houses. This kind of insult would sure deter members from indulging in crimes which may attract imprisonment for any term.

If a member is dismissed, By-elections cost several crores of Rupees to the exchequer. Under the present lopsided system of formation and dissolution of governments based on majority in the legislatures, the government may collapse if two or more members are disqualified. Opposition parties may form government or there may come midterm elections costing the exchequer thousands of crores of Rupees.

# 16

# Inequality, Is Only Political Mischief

Equality is sanctum Sanctorum under Bharathiya constitution since it is contained in the preamble as its objective and reiterated by Articles 14, 15, and 16. It is also natural justice that citizens of a country be treated equally at par with each other. We should also remember that every section of the society has fought for independence and made sacrifices.

Reverse discrimination is retribution and apartheid. We cannot discriminate any class with assumption that forefathers of that class, thousands of years ago, discriminated some other class.

We should remember, Bharath was not totally ruled by Bharathiyas during the last 1000 years. Majority of it was ruled by Christians and the Muslims for about a thousand years. Prior to their invading Bharath, today's backward classes were the rulers. Castes might have come in to existence due to formation of thousands of kingdoms after wars and aggressions. The winning class would naturally demeans the losing classes.

Discrimination is part of vote bank politics which congress party fully exploited. Communists tried to create the poor as their separate vote bank, but could not succeed. Unfortunate that though the constitution repeated thrice in Article 14, 15 and 16 as "the state shall not discriminate, the state shall not discriminate, the state shall not discriminate", the state is following "we discriminate, we discriminate, we discriminate". Most irresponsible leaders!

Independence was achieved after suffering discrimination for thousands of years at the hands of foreign rulers and with sacrifices of lacs of martyrs irrespective of their caste, creed, region, religion or sex. Independence is not achieved to discriminate people. Disunited people cannot make a united Bharath.

The British have handed over a large country to the native leaders. Native leaders, not having experience of ruling a country, much less a democratic country, divided the land in to linguistic states, Scheduled Areas and Jammu and Kashmir; divided the polity in to hundreds of political parties and divided the people on caste lines. In one word, they did everything that ought not to have been done under the constitution. Bharathiya leaders failed to forge fraternity and equality and to establish a Sovereign Democratic Republic.

It is also not true that Ambedkar provided for reservation in government employment separately for Scheduled Castes and Scheduled Tribes. Constitution provided only two types of reservations: 1) for

Scheduled Castes and Scheduled Tribes in legislatures, for 20 years, under Article 330 and 2) under Article 16 (4), in employment, to any backward class, if it is found to be not adequately represented in government employment, which includes Scheduled castes and Scheduled tribes if they are found to be not adequately represented in government employment, Giving of reservations to group of castes such as Scheduled Castes or Scheduled Tribes instead of individual castes, based on their population, is also illegal. Only the powerful castes in that group would enjoy at the cost of the weaker castes in that group. This kind of gross justice or gross injustice is jungle law. It led to struggles for classification of various groups of classes.

Article 16 is concerned with non-discrimination of citizen in matters of government jobs. Clause 4 of Article 16 reads, "Nothing in this article shall prevent the State from making any provision for the reservation of appointments or posts in favour of any backward class of citizens which, in the opinion of the State, is not adequately represented in the services under the State". This clause was sufficient to provide reservations in government jobs in favour of any backward class including Scheduled Castes and Scheduled Tribes.

Since this clause started with words "Provided that," we should understand that this clause should be used exceptionally but not generally. If it is used generally, it amounts to repealing of clauses (1) and (2) of Article 16 which emphasize non- discrimination of citizens based on caste, creed etc. in matters of government employment. It also militates against the very objective of equality of opportunities enshrined in the preamble. This clause is not a positive direction to the government to do or abstain from doing something like giving or not giving of reservations. It is like a permission which may or may not be utilised.

Any community, to get reservation under this clause, must fulfil two conditions namely,

1. to be included under list of backward classes and

2. must have been found not to be representing adequately in government jobs. This list must be compiled by the government separately which may include any caste in it. New castes may be added and existing castes omitted from this list by the government. Lot of caution was exercised in drafting this exemption lest it should violate the constitutional objective of equality of opportunities.

   What is use of these rhetoric objectives in the preamble and in the constitution if they do not come true even after seven decades of their being embedded in to the constitution? 70 years is unreasonably long period which cannot be considered normal under any circumstances. At least now the government should keep away from this kind of political game and gamble and strive to achieve real advancement of the backward classes without injuring the constitutional objective of equality of status and of opportunity among the citizens. Governments may discriminate people based on economic criteria but not based on their caste etc. Exact opposite of what is stated in the constitution is happening in Bharath as political tactics.

In ancient Bharath, there were only four varnas which were interchangeable. Women could acquire any upper varna by marriage while men could do that by personal achievement. There could be all the four varnas in the same family.

Ironically, even today, there are only four social strata namely S.C., S.T., B.C., and O.C. Any woman and her children can acquire the strata of her husband after marriage with him. As regards men, anybody can become a business man, a politician or a an Archaka, Purohit or a Religious Preacher by choice.

In due course of time, Four Varnas have become thousands of castes by forming their own kingdoms. As against this caste rule, as reform, successive kings adopted names such as Pallava, Chola, Pandya, Chera, Kakathiya and ruled those bigger kingdoms. When these bigger kingdoms fell to Mughals and Britishers, the common names disappeared and people again embraced their own castes. Thus, today's castes are not creeds, they are formed out of social, political and economic compulsions.

# 17

# SC., ST., BCs of Today Were Once Rulers

Major castes of S.C., S.T., and B.C.s of today were once rulers. It is logical to conclude that native tribes ruled over their own areas until intruded by others dislodging them from power and properties and degraded them as slaves. This is how thousands of kingdoms and castes could have been evolved. The winning group takes over the power, property and women of the defeated and kill, insult and enslave them. This is how disparities in various groups of people called castes could have evolved historically. It is a false theory that castes are formed based on means of livelihood.

Bharathiya culture and languages were nurtured by these native kings and all temples in Bharath were built only by them. All Bharathiya kings, Gods, saints and religious text writers belonged to them. They must have lost their riches, power and social importance, only after they lost their authority as rulers, in wars and aggressions. In due course, due to poverty and suffering, they lose memories of their past glory and start making livelihood by menial jobs as allowed by the winners. It was what happened everywhere in the world in human history. Some countries in the world returned to equality among people with emergence of democracy and able governments which has not happened in Bharath yet.

Kakatiyas belonged to Pulinda clan, a scheduled caste of today, who are known as "Boyas," who lived by hunting after losing their kingdoms. Andhra was ruled by Goudas at the time of Maha Bharata which dates to about 5300 years from now. The same community king by name Sarvai Papanna ruled over Telangana area just about 400 years back. They had to make livelihood thereafter, by toddy tapping for others. The kings who hung weights around neck of great Telugu Poet Srinadha, for not paying land rent, belonged to "Vodra" community who make livelihood now by undertaking manual earth works. Now, they are known as Vaddera. They ruled over Rayalaseema area of present Andhra Pradesh, about 400 years back.

Yadavas, who now breed sheep and cattle, belonged to caste of none other than Lord Srikrishna. Pandavas clan, we know, emanated from Vyas, the son of a fisher woman through a Brahmin Parasara. Nanda dynasty, founded by Mahapadma Nanda, belonged to barbers' community. Gonds, who are now Scheduled Tribes, once ruled kingdoms in Telangana and Madhya Pradesh. Salivahanas are said to be belonging to potter community of today. All maharajas of North Bharath like Mourya and Chouhans were Sudras. Not one, almost all kings of Bharath, East, West, North or South, were only Backward Classes of today from whom others have grabbed power by defeating them in wars. it is only after independence that the rich communities again have come to power through costly elections. Thus, Bharathiya political power percolated down from the B.C.s to Mughals to Britishers and to the present rich.

Scheduled Castes in several parts of Bharath call themselves as Jambavaths, which indicates that they were the original dwellers and rulers of Jamboo Dweep of which Bharath is a part. Administrations changed hands lacs of times ever since organized ruling has commenced in human communities. Rulers become down trodden and the down trodden become rules. It is an ongoing process yet.

The episode of Pandavas losing and gaining of their penny, power, people, women and respect has something to learn from. In the process of playing the deceitful game of dice, played for grabbing of kingdom from Pandavas, the Monarch Dharma Raj, first lost his wealth, followed by his kingdom, brothers, his wife and himself which led to their living in forests for 11 years and in slavery for one year under king Virat, in disguise. This is what happens to any ruling community when they lose power.

During these ordeals, they have not abdicated their Dharma as Kings. They honoured saints and prayed the Gods and gained blessings of all; they always protected the weak and stood up for justice. Five Pandavas alone have not fought back, though they were mighty as individuals. They met Kouravas in Kurukshetra with seven lacs of soldiers and other matching paraphernalia of war while the army of Duryodhan was 11 lacs.

It was possible for Pandavas only because they gained cooperation of so many other kings and communities. This is what the backward classes of today must learn. They should not abandon their own ancient Dharma. They should observe and protect it. If they fight in the name of their own caste, they may get pensions, rations and reservations but not political power to rule and regain their lost glory of the past.

Giving of one job in thousands of families of backward classes would not result in overall wellbeing of the entire community. Still, 95% of families of these communities remained under privileged without getting a government job in their family and they will remain so even after another several thousands of years, if the present lopsided system of reservations is continued. Backward classes are lured with jobs which are non-existent or insufficient in proportion to their population. It earned them more of envy of the poor in other communities than government jobs.

If there are differences in the rights and opportunities of people, based on caste, region, religion etc., fraternity among them will not survive, leave about flourishing of it. What is use of having the biggest written constitution unless it is followed?

Due to Prevention of Atrocities on S.C., S.T., Act, these communities are totally severed from rest of the society. From O.C.s and B.C.s, they do not get personal loans on promissory notes at times of need. They do not get residential accommodations for living or commercial accommodations to conduct business, on rent, lest Atrocities Act should be invoked by them on slightest deviation or demand for repayment of loan or for vacation of the property as per the rent agreement. They are not preferred even in private employment. It impairs their social living and earning opportunities and they would be relegated to their own colonies separated from main towns. People avoid making social and financial deals with them. Boys or girls from other communities would not be prepared to marry girls or boys from Scheduled Castes and Tribes for fear of being charged with atrocity even for small differences which are quite normal in families due to combined living. Thus, they are made totally dependent on the governmental help to live.

# 18

# Does Bharath Get Divided And Lose Independence?

There were demands in the past from several states like Assam, Punjab, Nagaland, Tripura, Manipur, Meghalaya, Mizoram etc., to sever them from Bharath. They were all militant movements and hence could be subdued with military power by Bharathiya government.

The situation at present is different. States are formed with separate linguistic identity with facility to have independent political parties, in the form of small and state parties, to make an organized demand for separation from Bharath.

At present, out of 29 states of Bharath, there are hardly 12 states in which national parties are in power exclusively without coalitions. Almost equal number of states are exclusively ruled by small and state parties. The rest of states are under coalitions with or without national parties in them. However, small and state parties are strong enough in each state to create disturbances with demands to separate them from the country.

If all the states like Telangana, Andhra, Tamil Nadu, Karnataka, Kerala, Maharashtra, Uttar Pradesh, Delhi, Bengal, Bihar, Orissa, Punjab, Jharkhand, Kashmir etc. states where small and state parties are strong, start making a concerted demand in the Parliament for bifurcation of the country, it would have grave impact on the political scenario in the country which is not far from now.

If they are not in sufficient majority in the Parliament to pass a bill for bifurcation of the country, still, they would encourage mass movements in the states with demand for bifurcation of the country. Violence, loot and arson would ensue in the states which will be dealt with lenience by regional governments in their states. Central government offices and institutions will be attacked with violence. National party leaders in states would be beaten up. Enemy countries take advantage of internal disturbances in Bharath and they, supply arms, ammunition, narcotics, money and training to the agitating groups. While the central government is engaged in battling with the rioters, infiltrations across the boarders will increase. These illegal migrants would be ready to respond with or without arms, at the call of their parent countries. They sneak in to the agitating mobs. The states which hitherto were not claiming to be separated also get attracted to the movement with possibility of division appearing imminent. International pressures would mount for honouring public opinion in the country which is manifested by the agitations. If these states go to election with demand for bifurcation of the country, national parties cannot even conduct election campaigns. They would lose deposits everywhere.

The small and state parties will pass resolutions in their respective assemblies. Regional governments would dissolve their assemblies and go for midterm elections in which they win with full majority which they show as public opinion. Regional party leaders would be regarded as heroes and protectors of regional interests while national parties and their leaders would be painted traitors and looters. People would be forced to take sides. It is high time that the problem of regionalism is nipped in the bud.

Reorganization of linguistic states, establishment of small and state parties, conflicts of caste, region, religion and language have sown the seed of separation of the country. The constitutional framers consciously prohibited discrimination of citizens based on caste, community, creed, region, religion and language. Unfortunately, small and state political parties are mushrooming only to propagate the prohibited issues.

Bharath may even lose independence, if bifurcated. Foreign corporates have already entered Bharath with view to capture Bharathiya economy which would eventually lead to command over all aspects of administration of the country. People are frustrated to the maximum over state of affairs in the country. People are already accepting foreign goods and services for their quality. Whoever have opportunity, are eager to leave the country.

It appears, the Bharathiya rulers have not learnt lessons from the past. Even today, all the ill traits of jealousy, corruption, disunity, luxuries are persisting in Bharathiya rulers, of course, in a greater measure. These disunited, jealous and selfish Bharathiya leaders, who ignored the written constitution of the country, cannot defend the country for long, against external armed invasions or external commercial aggressions or internal rebellion. They are not able to at least establish a proper government in accordance with the constitution so far.

Sovereignty is an essential characteristic of any country which is missing in Bharath. There is not a single government that can rule over entire country. There are about 30 independent and mutually conflicting governments in Bharath in the form of state and central governments. One Chief Minister says, he would not obey the Prime Minister's advices, another says he would not implement Acts passed by the Parliament, some other Chief Minister dares Prime Minister to enter his state, some other says he would not allow central law enforcing authorities in to his state, yet another, calls him names. Prime Minister enacts dignity and remains silent on being affronted by his political opponents because he really does not have Constitutional authority to act against them except foisting of some false or genuine cases of crime or corruption on them through use or misuse of his administrative influence over central investigating agencies.

There are external aggressions from all sides of the country and internal disturbances everywhere in the country. There are several people in Bharath who are eager to become traitors. As such we cannot guarantee that the country would not lose independence once again in a near future unless drastic institutional changes take place in Bharath. How long Bharath can remain independent, without an honoured constitution and an effective sovereign authority to defend it, is to be seen.

Previously, there was only one East India Company operating in Bharath while at present, hundreds of such companies have descended on Bharath due to globalization of trade and industry. Roads and other infrastructure in Bharath are built with foreign loans as stipulated by the foreign lenders to suit their needs. Local enterprises being unable to compete with these global firms in terms of capital, infrastructure, technology, manpower and scales of operations would bow out from competition. The whole country becomes dependent on foreign trading firms for supply of goods and services. Governments would be forced to facilitate their business operations at the behest of W.T.O., and other international organizations and foreign governments.

Governments get proper taxes without evasion from these big foreign firms, rather than from lacs of local retailers. These foreign trading firms will also provide funds for the political parties and the politicians individually. They would also take political sides and influence Bharathiya politics. As a result, Bharathiya politicians vie with each other to facilitate the businesses of foreign firms. Bharathiya natural resources would be made available to them at thrown away price. The main job of our governments would be to protect and facilitate the businesses of the foreign corporate firms from agitating mobs. They make laws for that purpose. These foreign business firms can corrupt the bureaucrats and the politicians at high levels to get things done in their favour.

Foreign banks, insurance companies, hospitals, hotels and universities are being allowed in to Bharath. Foreign Direct Investment is allowed without any limit in most of the sectors including defence. They can take over Bharathiya companies through purchase of shares from the share market. The local units are already feeling the heat and are at the verge of extinction.

Who intend to get benefited out of trade in Bharath, praise Bharath to be the largest market for their products and forecast Bharath to become a super power in the next twenty years to come. Local leaders woo the voters with forecasts of transforming their respective regions in to golden or heavenly. Both the foreign as well as regional leaders know it to be a hoax. Development of a geographic area is different from development of the people of that area. Even if Bharath or any of its states become golden, or heaven like, the people living in that area would be foreigners but not any native sons of soil. Native

Bharathiyas would be driven away, killed or enslaved and annihilated in due course.

Regional governments allot huge extent of lands to the foreign firms who will naturally build lavish infrastructure on such lands. There, would come up wide roads and high-rise buildings which give a misleading impression of development. Beautiful hotels, malls, modern bars and restaurants will come up in the vicinity and luxurious cars would be running on the roads. This is a look like development which would not benefit the lives of local people except affecting their lives with pollution. The development which is brought about by encouraging local entrepreneurs, use of local raw material and deployment of local man power and local tourism and self-employment alone would help the balanced and simultaneous growth of the local people and local area.

Some people boast of Bharath as having the largest contingent of employable youth in the world. Bharathiya leaders, quoting the foreign nationals, announce vision 2020, 2030, 2040 etc. by which they make Golden Bharath, Diamond Bharath or Platinum Bharath. Innocent citizens get elated. Intelligent party leaders pretend to be believing, but the truth remains the same. Bharath was developing nation when I was studying 10th class in 1972 and it continues be the same even now in 2022.

It would be a proud moment for Bharath if the country were capable of supplying goods and services manufactured in Bharath to the world whereby it becomes rich like a developed nation. Instead, our educated youth are leaving for other countries for a better life which is not something to be proud of. They are leaving the country only because they have no opportunities here. Old parents suffer due to departure of their sons and daughters who are supposed to look after them in their old age. It does not amount to supply of goods or services to other countries except supplying of manpower to other countries, which we lose permanently.

Bharath is endowed with the best of natural resources like forests, fertile lands, rivers, lakes, hill stations, snowy mountains, minerals and sea shores. It has the largest contingent of employable youth. People are hardworking and law abiding. It abounds in tourism spots, history and mythology. It can be a devotional and historical tourism centre for many people, many countries and many faiths. There are many capable leaders in Bharath. Bharathiya police and bureaucrats are highly capable. We have all the things required to make one of the best countries in the world. What we lack is a proper system. In the absence of a good system, all the good traits of the country are going under the drain.

The first-round of sufferers, due to globalization of trade and industry, without strengthening the local trade and industry, will be the poor and next is the middle class followed by the rich. The rich would become poor within no time, unnoticed and inevitably. The corporate firms start catering to the needs of the rich in the country. Prices of consumer goods and services will go up making lives of poor, miserable. Even agricultural seeds, which germinate only once, we have to buy from these firms. Thus, even food in Bharath would be controlled by these firms. People would not be able to revolt being poor and helpless. Small political parties, or revolutionary political parties which are not financially supported by these corporate firms, would not be able to organize mass agitations. People would be forced to live in submission or die.

Local governments, being unable to afford reasonable standard of living to the masses would give them freedom, under the advices of these foreign corporate firms, to brew and consume illicit liquor, use of narcotics, pornography, prostitution and gambling and all sorts of vices to render them substandard and useless and die pre matured. Fertility of people will come down. New born babies will be under weighed and suffer malnutrition. Mothers would not be able to breast feed their children due to debility. People cannot afford medical facilities due to poverty and they sell their organs for money. Foreign hospitals in Bharath would fleece the rich who come to them for treatment and within a short period, Bharathiya population would be reduced to half. People ignore their culture and values, do not hesitate to live in crime, begging or through immoral activities.

The police will take stern action under the instructions of the governments at the behest of the foreign corporate firms and even shoot down the agitators who obstruct financial operations of foreign firms. Special courts and tribunals would be established to deal with those who participate in agitations. Thus, in one word, the rule would be of an economic dictatorship by foreign business firms in Bharath. Bharathiya politicians would just act as their agents. This is what the object of the present-day international politics, unlike the earlier day politics of territorial acquisitions by beheading the enemy kings. They only siphon out the resources of countries and make them useless while enriching their own countries through trade, commerce and industry.

The governments would be forced to sell or mortgage on long-term basis of its strategic locations like airports, seaports, road ways, railways or telecommunications in favour of foreign enterprises or foreign governments in satisfaction of loans payable to them. It happened in several third world countries. Sri Lanka had to part with possession of Humbathoti, a strategic naval base, to China on 100 years lease in satisfaction of a debt of about 1.2 billion dollars in 2018. They still owed about 8 billion to China. Imagine how many airports, sea ports, and industries Srilanka must pledge for the remaining 8 billion dollars.

# 19

# Suicides of The Poor, A Genocide

Small and uneconomic land holdings, non availability of parallel sources of earnings to these farmers, rigid land tenancy laws which restricted the moment of farmers to other areas or in to other means of livelihood, and delay in delivery of justice trough courts are the root causes of suicides of small and marginal farmers and the poor in Bharath which has never been understood and addressed by the successive governments. Instead, they tried to woo this large chunk of voters to vote them by offering temporary monitory benefits.

In the name of land reforms, agricultural lands from the big farmers who held more than 40 acres, were taken over by the government under Land Ceiling Act and distributed 3 to 5 Acres each to the landless poor families which created uneconomic land holdings. This is a socialistic pattern adopted by Nehru against the constitution to stall socialistic and communistic movements in Bharath. Factors of production were divided affecting the productivity. Instead, produce should have been controlled by governmental laws, to benefit the poor and the farm labour. We should remember, Ambedkar has incorporated property right as one of the fundamental rights. Congress government changed it as constitutional right under Article 300A which ought not to have been violated so freely. This is mainly responsible for suicides of lacs of farmers and the poor. The very nature of landed properties is to get divided among successors of successive generations. Within no time, each land holding has come down to the size of 1 to 2 acres. Agriculture has become uneconomical resulting in deaths of lacs of people.

Income from a land holding of 2 acres would be around Rs. 30000 per annum, which gives an average monthly income of Rs. 2500. This is much below the poverty line income. How a farmer can support his family with this meagre income? He tries to raise commercial crops and earn more in his limited land holding or he may take some other land on lease. Commercial crops may yield more income, but their investment is also more. The Law of Diminishing Returns would come in to play; the land loses its natural quality, becomes infertile, the crops suffer due to usage of excessive fertilizers and pesticides. The farmer borrows money for buying seeds, fertilizers and pesticides. He digs a bore well and purchases pump sets etc. Sometimes, he may not find water in the bore well. The threat of pests is also more in commercial crops. The prices of the yield fluctuate wildly. Being unable to bear the losses, he commits suicide.

At least Fifty lakh of the poor and the farmers must have committed suicides during the last 75 years in the country yet, the governments have not come out with a viable solution for the suicides of farmers. Out of these numbers, at least 95% are farmers of less than 3 Acres or lease hold farmers.

Successive governments have declared various incentives to the farmers such as Rs. 50 per unit of electricity for farm supply, Free Power, loan waiver, Rythu Bandhu etc. All these schemes applied to the small and big farmers alike resulting in waste of government money. Some are using this facility even for farm houses. Big farmers benefited the big way while the small farmers got a pittance. A farmer of 2 Acres gets electricity concession of about Rs. 3000 per annum, loan waiver of Rs. 20000 and Rytu Bandhu of Rs. 20000 while a farmer's family of 3 members and 30 Acres gets 45000 on electricity, Rs. 300000 loan waiver and Rs. 300000 on account of Rythu Bandhu. Such schemes are intelligent plans devoid of humanity, justice and fair play, with knowledge that big farmers control the villages.

A small farmer is committing suicide being unable to repay a debt of about Rs. 3 lakhs on an average. What is use of giving Rs. 6 lakhs to his kin after his death? Many families are deprived of this benefit too. Since the head of family has died, the uneducated, worried, wife and her small children cannot pursue the case to get the benefit. Officials anyhow, search reasons to avoid the payment on the ground that it is not suicide for agricultural reasons.

The governments should accept responsibility if people are unable to live in the society created by it, as it takes credit for the development. A farmer may die of heart failure looking at his parched farm due to lack of water or due to pests. He may die of mental tension thinking how to repay the debt, how to face the creditors, how to perform his daughter's marriage and how to support educational and medical needs of his family. He may become alcoholic due to tensions and die languishing. He may die of an electric shock or a snake bite at night in his field. If we term all such deaths as not relating to agriculture, there is no more sin than this.

Even the opposition parties are not serious about it except demanding for more facilities for the farming community and for better support prices. As discussed above, all such measures would help big and small farmers alike, but cannot prevent suicides of small and marginal farmers. If the government really wants a solution for the problems of suicides of small and marginal farmers, it could have found it so easily because the target group is defined in terms of extent of holding and indebtedness. The government could have constituted committees to study the debt problems of farmers and settle the debts with the creditors pro-rata from a rotating rescue fund. It would have been better for the farmers and the creditors as well. The farmer gets back his securities and lives in peace.

The governments are distributing trucks, tractors etc. to rich farmers. Instead, without asking for down payment, they should be given to the small and marginal farmers who could find a new and parallel source of earning. They are suffering disguised unemployment due to their small holding. If new implements or equipment are given to them, they can use them for earning income after their own agricultural operations are completed. The government can waive the down payment because, it already earned taxes on such equipment.

Construction of dams and canals beyond requirement would worsen the situation because of two reasons: one, though the project is constructed by spending lakhs of crores on it, the average holding of a farmer under the project is only 3 Acres. Probably, he could be earning Rs. 30000 per annum before he had water facility and after that facility, he may earn another Rs. 20000 which cannot prevent his suicide. What he needs is at least Rs. 2.5 lakhs income per year to be above the poverty line.

Over production of agricultural produce too is harmful due to law of demand and supply. If supply is more than the demand, there would not be takers for the agricultural products and they do not fetch economic prices in the market. We are witnessing: in many places where farmers abandon their crops without harvesting due to harvesting and transporting costs being more than the prices of their products in the markets.

Tenancy laws, besides land reforms, are responsible for suicides of farmers. In the past, tenants were granted pattas for lands which they were cultivating as lease hold farmers. Even today, the law is that one cannot vacate a tenant farmer even if he does not pay the lease amount. Land lords are not inclined to lease their small holding for fear of losing it. It curtails migration of small farmers in to other trades or other areas where they can find better livelihood. Neither could they live depending on agriculture in such lands. They stick on to their uneconomical land holding. Natural outcome is suicides. In the name of reforms and help, governments are killing people.

# 20

# National Parties Are Fighting Losing Battle

The fight between national parties and small and state parties in the elections is a fight between two un equals, one armed with appropriate weapons and the other with inappropriate weapons, which is unfair. The national parties should grow wiser and understand that they are fighting with an incompatible weapon with that in the hands of small and state parties. They are bound to lose the battle and disappear in the states where the small and state parties come to exist in the present political format.

The small and state parties are armed with departments which deal with items in state list under the constitution such as law and order, irrigation, agriculture, education, electricity, medical care, social welfare, mining, roads and buildings, housing and municipalities which touch the lives of people day in and day out, apart from own print and electronic media in local language, while national parties are armed with national subjects such as monetary policy, defence, banking, international relations and direct taxes etc., which are not so directly discerned by state citizens. On the contrary, national parties would be blamed for all the problems of the state. The state governments implement welfare schemes and take credit for them. People do not know the contribution of the centre in the welfare schemes implemented by the states. The states brand them as theirs.

The regional party governments can intimidate national party leaders and cadre existing in the states. They can just stifle the life of any person living in that state. National party leaders in states where small and state parties are in power have to live in fear. This is also the reason why national parties cannot hold their feet in the states where small and state parties have firm ground. National party leaders and cadre migrate to small and state parties for survival and support. People also cannot support national parties openly in such states for fear of being targeted by the regional governments.

When narrow considerations of caste, creed, religion, region, language etc. enter the minds of people, they defy all law and logic which will eventually lead to claiming a separate country for their region. The small and state parties would also advance a convincing argument that there are several countries in the world, which are smaller than a state in Bharath and yet surviving and flourishing like most advanced nations. They would also remind the people of their state being independent country before the Mughals or the Britishers occupied it or just before it was merged with Bharathiya union after independence. People would also accept such arguments with hope of ending their sufferings. They would consider anything as better than the present situation.

The regional governments would also impress upon the people in the state that they want to implement more and more welfare schemes for different sections of the state. They lament that the centre is taking away all the revenues of the state and returning only a pittance which is crippling the financial strength of their state. They blame that the central government is callous to their sufferings. People would be moved and become prepared to die or kill. This is the first step in mentally preparing the people of a state to accept claim for a separate country.

Regional political parties would spend whole of their state resources on welfare schemes while neglecting the developmental projects which need investment. They know, poverty of the people is the necessary input for their politics. People are purposefully kept poor so that they would be dependent on the governments for survival in the form of welfare schemes from the governments and the notes to be distributed by the political parties in the elections. They can also demand huge funds from the union for social welfare schemes and for relief works at times of natural calamities and blame the union government for not extending adequate help to the states. They do not disclose to beneficiaries of the share of union government in welfare schemes.

The best example of strength of regionalism is the political disaster, the Congress party faced in Telugu states after bifurcation of the state into Andhra Pradesh and Telangana in 2014. Neither people of Telangana honoured it for giving a separate state nor Andhra Pradesh people showed gratitude for giving them a separate state for which both the states agitated in the past. Neither death of Rajiv Gandhi in Tamil Nādu nor giving of a separate state for Andhra and Telangana could change the minds of voters in those states, whose minds are marshalled by small and state parties and regional feeling.

Terrorists from small neighbouring country, Sri Lanka, could assassinate the former Bharathiya Prime Minister Rajiv Gandhi while he was on an election campaign in Tamil Nādu, only because there was a regional government in that state at that time. It was a law-and-order failure in that state which was responsible for his assassination. The state government should have been dissolved and the President's rule imposed under Article 352 or 356 in Tamil Nādu consequent to assassination of Rajiv Gandhi. It could not be done because the government at the centre, which emerged after elections, was a coalition government which could not incur the wrath of small and state parties who may stand united in solidarity. His assassination during 1991 general elections even did not influence the voting pattern in the country or within that state, post the incident, only because the person killed belonged to a national party and the government in that state was headed by a regional party.

To keep their vote bank united under some solidarity, small and state parties would always be inciting the people of their state against central government and governments of neighbouring states on one pretext or the other leading to loss of fraternity and patriotism in the hearts of people which, one day, would lead to demanding to sever their state from the country to form a country of their own. The unlimited freebies and the resultant backwardness of the state would fuel the fire.

Regional political parties establish their own print and electronic media units in vernacular language to propagate positive news about them. These parties would support the media units by way of advertisements from private patrons and the government. These biased channels will transmit malevolent and mendacious news to mould public opinion in favour of their patronizing political parties and to malign their opposition parties. These media units flood the people with false impressions rather than information regarding facts. Small and state parties do not encourage use of national link languages in their states to spread because they do not want people of their states to understand and get influenced by national leaders and national news. Tamil Nādu is much ahead in this aspect in comparison to other states.

Regional political parties are established by rich and influential communities in states. Their own caste people would lend support in terms of men and money in anticipation of political positions and contracts to their community people after their party coming to power. These parties compete among themselves to woo support of S.C., S.T., B.C., communities and religious minorities who are major stock of voters for any political party. In their effort to come to power, they offer various benefits to these people on caste lines whether they really needed or not, without concern for national fraternity, unity and integrity.

Unwanted, unsolicited, unnecessary freebees, distributed at the cost of development of the state, will bankrupt the treasury and in due course lead to utter poverty, crime and corruption in the state. Politicians start criticizing each other for the fiasco. People also take sides, unable to trace the true cause of their sufferings.

# 21

# States Are Alienating Lands Without Authority

List 1 of 7<sup>th</sup> schedule to the constitution enumerates subjects on which the union government alone can make laws. List 2 is the state list and List 3 is the concurrent list on which both, state and centre may make law. However, parliament made laws take precedence over the state made laws on items included in List 3. Entry 18 of List 2 reads, "Land, that is to say, rights in or over land, land tenures including the relation of landlord and tenant, and the collection of rents; transfer and alienation of agricultural land; land improvement and agricultural loans; colonization".

"Transfer and alienation of agricultural land" means the process involving transfers and alienations affected through registrations and the stamp duty leviable on such transactions which take place between private land sellers and buyers. It gives right to states to regulate by law, land ownership and transfer by the private individuals. Comprehensive reading of this entry lets us to know that the lands are not owned by states and that they cannot alienate them. It is not meant to authorise the state governments to sell away government lands to others. State governments are not owners of lands in the states and hence, they cannot sell lands. Further, this entry speaks of agricultural lands, but not non-agricultural lands. Lists 1, 2 and 3 only enlists subjects on which states and the centre can make laws. It does not mean that states and centre can sell away whatever mentioned in their list. If we agree that state councils of ministers have right to sell an inch of the land obtaining in the states, it amounts to accepting that they can sell away the whole state. The state governments acquire lands at government prices from the formers for public use and sell lands in their possession through auctions, at huge cost. It is an unethical practice. Such a procedure is not laid down under any law. Governments cannot acquire private lands except for public purpose. Thus, governments cannot hold lands but for public purpose. Governments must return lands in their possession to the original owners from whom they were acquired or to their legal heirs.

The councils of ministers headed by Chief Ministers are exercising rights which they do not have under the constitution. Generally, it is the Chief Minister who holds the sway over the decisions of the council of ministers. Generally, he is also the head of the party who provides tickets and funds for the contestants. As such, the party head goes to any extent to gain and retain power. If regional leaders know that it is the President appointed Governor who holds executive power of state and not the Chief

Minister and that state councils of ministers do not have right to alienate lands in the state, they would not have sacrificed their businesses and earning sources to pursue politics as their full-time career. In fact, they are supposed to execute such of the duties which are entrusted to them by the Governors. Instead, they are bypassing the willing Governors and taking upon themselves the whole administration of the state under mistaken feeling of federalism. President is the fiduciary owner and guardian of entire territory of Union of Bharath. He should ensure unity and integrity of it. That is also the reason why the President is termed Supreme Commander of Armed Forces under Article 53.

The right given to states over lands under Entry 18, List 2, is only user of the lands and their administration but not to sell them away. Right to sell lands, or the procedures to follow in such transactions, is not contained under entry 18, List 2.

The right of state governments relating to lands existing in the states is like that of trustees over trust properties. Or, it may be compared to rights of head of a joint family over the family properties standing in his name. Without permission of the Parliament and the President, none can sell government lands in Bharath, much less the state ministers.

If all the lands in states belong to the states with right to alienate them, where shall the central government stand? Can we say that the central government does not have right to land in Bharath?

Since, the entry "Lands" is contained in List 2, states have right to make laws regarding lands. But such making of law should not take out the lands from the control of the states.

If state ministers have right to alienate the landed properties in the states, they may alienate all the lands of the state in favour of their own friends and family members and foreign corporate firms for personal profit. If these foreign corporates, after being allotted lands to them, experience even the slightest inconvenience in utilizing these lands, the international trade organizations and the native countries of these foreign corporate firms will even attack Bharath. Alienating parts of state lands is like losing of sovereignty phase wise.

Each Constitutional authority in the country undertakes in its oath of office to respect the Sovereignty, unity and Integrity of the country. Despite so much loud and clear objective of the Constitution and oaths of constitutional authorities, different governments are formed in different states by different political parties, defying the Sovereignty and they are indiscriminately alienating state lands in favour of even foreign corporate firms as quid pro quo. Land has become the major source of corruption in the states.

It was what happened before Bharath lost independence to the British. In 1773 or so, the Nawab of Bengal allotted Diwani rights to East India Company whereby the Company acquired rights to collect land revenue from three states namely Orissa, Bihar and Bengal. Later, the Company requested the Nawab to give permission for establishment of their own civil courts and limited police force to deal with people who are in relationship with the Company. The law and order and landed properties of the country went in to the hands of the Company. What transpired thereafter is knowledge of all of us. The same thing is happening today in the states. There is need to control it forth with. Or else, there will be exclusive areas for the American, Chinese, Pakistan, Bangladesh, or any other foreign corporate firms on Bharathiya soil.

www.ingramcontent.com/pod-product-compliance
Lightning Source LLC
Chambersburg PA
CBHW051103250726
48656CB00001B/445